FORGE
YOUR INNER
STRENGTH

THE SECRETS TO TRANSFORM YOU INTO A PERSON OF STRENGTH PURPOSE AND LASTING JOY

William M. James

Table of Contents

Introduction 1

My First Step Into Strength 2

How I Decided To Shape My Life 3

Tools That Helped Me Will Help You 4

Discovering Inner Awareness 7

What Is Inner Awareness? 12

Daily Mindfulness Practices 21

Building a Foundation of Self-Reflection 28

Core Values and Purpose 37

Uncovering Your Core Values 40

Setting Goals with Your Values 46

Finding Purpose and Meaning 54

Developing Resilient Habits 61

The Power of Habit Reprogramming 65

Building Lasting Positive Habits 73

Intentionality in Everyday Actions 81

Cultivating Emotional Resilience 91

Emotional Resilience Explained 95

Managing Stress and Anxiety Tools 104

Overcoming Obstacles with a Growth Mindset 113

Building Authentic Relationships 121

The Value of Connection 124

Strengthening Key Relationships 132

Creating Boundaries, Protecting Energy 138

Gratitude and Positive Thinking 145

Cultivating a Grateful Mindset 148

Reframing Negative Thoughts 155

Building Positivity Daily 163

Sustaining Growth and Transformation 171

Embracing Lifelong Growth 175

Personal Empowerment Plan 183

Finding Support and Accountability 191

Conclusion 199

Key Insights and Practices Recap 201

The Journey Forward 203

Resources for Learning and Growth 206

The Phases of Personal Growth 208

Pioneers in Personal Growth 211

Earl Nightingale: The Power of Thought and Purpose 212

Napoleon Hill: The Power of Desire and Faith 214

Norman Vincent Peale: Positive Thinking for Fulfillment 216

Jim Rohn: Personal Responsibility and Character-Building 218

Zig Ziglar: Motivation and Faith-Based Success 220

Brian Tracy: Goal-Setting and Time Management 222

Bob Proctor: The Law of Attraction and Self-Belief 224

Conclusion: A Legacy of Inner Strength and Success 226

Introduction
A Choice To Rise

I n today's world, where pressures are constant and distractions seem endless, finding true peace and resilience within ourselves can feel almost impossible. Like many, I spent years trying to keep up with the demands of life, often feeling like I was running in circles without real direction or purpose. This all changed during a defining period in my life, following the sudden loss of a close friend. I remember the shock and sadness, the overwhelming grief that seemed impossible to face. When life confronts us with hardship, it's natural to retreat, to let fear and sadness define our reactions. But in those weeks after the loss, I realized I had a choice: I could let grief control my life, or I could make the bold decision to find strength and purpose within myself.

The concepts in this book emerged from my own path of growth and self-discovery. I began to notice how even the smallest changes—practices of mindfulness, intentional actions, and meaningful connections—helped me rebuild myself. At the time, I didn't fully realize the impact these practices would have, but as I committed to them, my life gradually transformed. I became more grounded, resilient, and focused. This experience taught me that inner strength isn't something we're simply born with; it's something we actively build. *Forge Your Inner Strength* is the guide I wish I'd had when I first set out on this path. Each chapter introduces concepts and practices that helped me overcome challenges and discover a deeper purpose, and I hope they will do the same for you. Many people hesitate to look deeply within themselves because they fear what they might find. It's uncomfortable to question our choices, our habits, and our reactions. I felt the same, but I found that as I grew in self-awareness, I gained a profound sense of peace and clarity. In this book, I've included exercises and reflections that simplify these concepts, helping you explore your own inner strength in a way that feels approachable and impactful.

At the end of the book, I've also included a chapter dedicated to the wisdom of some of the most influential thinkers in the field of personal growth. Their timeless lessons on resilience, positivity, and purpose have shaped the foundation of self-improvement, and their insights served as guiding lights in my own path. I hope this chapter inspires you to explore these ideas and draw from the wisdom of these pioneers, just as I have.

My First Step Into Strength

My journey toward inner strength truly began with a single, life-changing decision in the days after my friend's passing. One evening, in the quiet of my room, I sat alone, looking at an old photograph of us together, and I felt completely lost. I remember wondering who I was without the presence of this person in my life. In that moment, I realized that if I wanted to keep moving forward, I would need to find an anchor within myself. Like most people, I'd often let external factors define my happiness, letting people, situations, or possessions guide my feelings of worth and purpose. But sitting there, I decided I wanted to go deeper, to forge a strength that no loss or setback could ever take away from me.

Making this decision felt like stepping into unknown territory. Many of us are hesitant to step outside our comfort zones, to confront our fears or change our routines, even if those routines aren't serving us. But taking that first step, uncomfortable as it was, felt freeing. I committed to small, intentional practices that helped me reconnect with myself—journaling, practicing gratitude, and spending time in nature. Each of these habits felt small, almost insignificant at the time, but gradually, they became the foundation for a more fulfilled, purposeful life.

This book invites you to make similar choices, embracing challenges and adopting habits that align with your true self. Like me, you'll find that each step toward building your inner strength brings you closer to a life that reflects your deepest values and aspirations. In the process, you'll discover that every experience, even the painful ones, can become a stepping stone toward a stronger, more authentic you.

How I Decided To Shape My Life

Losing someone close was an experience that changed my outlook on life, revealing the power of intentional change in a way nothing else had. In those early days, I often felt like life was happening to me, that I was at the mercy of my emotions. Many of us share this reaction—when faced with difficulty, we tend to blame circumstances or let external situations control our reactions. But I realized that if I wanted to live a life of purpose, I would have to make mindful, intentional changes in my thoughts, habits, and actions.

One day, during a particularly low moment, I took a walk to clear my head. As memories came flooding in, I chose to focus on gratitude rather than grief. It was a small shift in perspective, but it opened my eyes to the possibility of using each decision as a tool for growth. I began to actively shape my thoughts and routines, choosing positivity over negativity, gratitude over sorrow. By doing this daily, I started to feel more grounded, confident, and resilient.

Intentional change became my lifeline, and it's now a central concept in this book. Each chapter will guide you in embracing small, mindful choices that will ripple through your life, gradually transforming both your inner world and outer reality. I can't promise that it will always be easy—embracing intentional change is challenging, as it often means releasing familiar habits and comfort zones. But as you begin to make these shifts, you'll find the strength to reshape your life in ways that reflect your values and bring a sense of deep fulfillment.

Tools That Helped Me Will Help You

I've structured this book to be your travelling companion, guiding you through each step of empowerment and personal growth. Each chapter combines concepts, exercises, and prompts that I discovered and refined via my personal experience. These tools are designed to resonate with your experiences, encouraging you to adapt them to your unique needs and goals.

When I was on my own journey of healing and growth, I made it a point to record each insight, each small breakthrough. I'd encourage you to do the same as you read this book. Give yourself the space to explore each chapter fully. Reflect on the exercises, journal your thoughts, and remember that growth takes time. The insights you gain won't come all at once but will emerge as you progress through each chapter, gradually building your inner strength.

I also learned that sharing my progress with a trusted friend added another level of meaning and accountability. I encourage you to share your road to recovery with someone close to you. Not only will it deepen your understanding of the concepts, but it will create a support system that makes the process feel more engaging. You may find yourself returning to certain chapters as your perspective shifts, and that's okay— growth is rarely linear, and each time you revisit a concept, it may reveal something new.

Ultimately, I hope that *Forge Your Inner Strength* provides you with the same tools, insights, and encouragement that I received along the way. I invite you to approach these pages with an open mind, compassion for yourself, and the knowledge that true strength is built, day by day, choice by choice. Accept this journey as a chance to know yourself better, to connect with what truly matters, and to cultivate the resilience and peace that are already within you.

Kick-Off Exercise: Goal setting for Personal Growth Exercise

Objective: Clarify personal goals and set intentions for your journey through the book.

Type: Reflection and Goal-Setting Exercise

Duration: One-time session, for at least 30-45 minutes.

Instructions:

1. Set Aside Time: Dedicate 30-45 minutes for this exercise. Choose a time when you can reflect deeply without interruptions.

2. Find a Quiet Space: Choose a calm and comfortable place where you won't be disturbed.

3. Reflection and Goal-Setting Prompts: Answer the following prompts to clarify your personal goals and set intentions:

   - *Identify Areas for Growth*: Reflect on different areas of your life (e.g., career, relationships, health, personal development). Write down specific areas where you want to experience growth.

   - *Clarify Personal Goals*: For each area identified, write down specific, achievable goals. Ensure these goals are SMART (Specific, Measurable, Achievable, Relevant, Time-bound).

   - *Set Intentions*: Write down your intentions for achieving these goals. Consider the mindset and behaviors you need to adopt to support your growth.

   - *Action Plan*: Outline a brief action plan for each goal. Identify the steps you need to take, any resources or support you might need, and a timeline for achieving these steps.

   - *Visualize Success*: Take a few moments to visualize yourself achieving these goals. Imagine the positive impact on your life and how you will feel once you have accomplished them.

4. Document Your Reflections: Use a notebook, a digital document, or a journaling app to record your reflections and goals. This will help you track your progress over time and reinforce your commitment to personal growth.

Discovering Inner Awareness

I nner awareness is the cornerstone of personal growth and a pivotal element in forging a resilient and joyful life. It involves a deep dive into the core of our being, understanding our thoughts, emotions, and the subtle undercurrents that influence our actions and reactions. At its essence, inner awareness is about cultivating a mindful relationship with oneself, a process that requires patience, curiosity, and a willingness to confront both our strengths and vulnerabilities. This adventure of self-discovery empowers us to live more authentically, making decisions that align with our true values and aspirations.

The first step towards developing inner awareness is to become an observer of your own mind. Eckart Tolle, in his famous book *The Power of Now* wrote '*Realize deeply that the present moment is all you ever have*'. This means paying attention to your thoughts and feelings without judgment or immediate reaction. Imagine sitting by a river and watching leaves float by; similarly, observe your thoughts as they come and go.

This practice can be challenging, as it goes against our natural tendency to engage with every thought emotionally or analytically. However, with consistent practice, you will begin to notice patterns in your thinking, including habitual thoughts that may not serve your highest good.

Understanding mindfulness and self-awareness is crucial in this regard. Mindfulness is the practice of being present and fully engaged with the moment, without distraction or judgment. By incorporating mindfulness into your daily routine, you can enhance your capacity for inner awareness. Simple activities such as mindful breathing, eating, or walking can serve as gateways to a more profound sense of presence and self-awareness. These practices help quiet the mind, making space for a deeper connection with the self.

The role of thoughts in shaping your life cannot be overstated. Our thoughts influence our emotions, decisions, and ultimately, the quality of our lives. By becoming more aware of our thought patterns, we can begin to identify those that are constructive and those that are limiting or destructive. This awareness is the first step toward changing negative thought patterns and fostering a more positive, empowering mindset. In the book *You Can Heal Your Life* Louise Hay wrote '*You have been criticizing yourself for years, and it hasn't worked. Try approving of yourself and see what happens*'.

To facilitate this process, daily mindfulness practices are invaluable. Morning thought journaling, for instance, can provide insight into your subconscious mind, revealing underlying beliefs and assumptions that shape your perception of reality. This practice involves writing down your thoughts as soon as you wake up, without censorship or judgment. Over time, this can reveal recurring themes and patterns, offering clues to your inner world and how it influences your external reality.

Observing thoughts without judgment is another critical practice in developing inner awareness. It involves detaching from your thoughts and emotions, viewing them as separate from your core self. This doesn't mean suppressing or ignoring your thoughts but rather allowing them to be without becoming entangled in them. This practice can be challenging but is incredibly liberating, as it helps you realize that you are not your thoughts or emotions; you are the awareness behind them.

It's crucial to approach this experience with an open heart and mind as we go deeper into the investigation of inner awareness. The process of self-discovery is unique to each individual, and what works for one person may not work for another. Therefore, it's crucial to explore various practices and techniques to find what resonates with you. Remember, the goal is not to achieve perfection but to cultivate a deeper understanding and connection with yourself. This ongoing process is both the challenge and the reward of developing inner awareness, laying the foundation for a life of authenticity, resilience, and fulfillment.

Building a foundation of self-reflection is another vital step in nurturing inner awareness. This involves regularly taking time to reflect on your experiences, feelings, and reactions. Self-reflection can be facilitated through practices such as meditation, journaling, or even quiet contemplation. These moments of introspection allow you to connect with your inner self, understand your motivations, and recognize the alignment or misalignment of your actions with your core values. Through self-reflection, you can also identify negative patterns that might be holding you back, such as self-doubt, fear, or procrastination. Recognizing these patterns is the first step in transforming them.

Positive visualization and affirmations play a significant role in reinforcing a positive mindset and self-image. Visualization involves picturing a desired outcome or state of being, engaging all your senses to make the experience as real as possible. This practice can effectively reprogram your subconscious mind, aligning your thoughts and energy with your goals and aspirations. Maxwell Maltz, author of *Psycho-Cybernetics*, highlighted this by stating, '*Visualize the person you want to be and then act as if you already are that person*'. By aligning your mindset with your desired outcomes, visualization and affirmations can reshape your inner narrative, leading to improved self-esteem and a more optimistic outlook on life.

Recognizing negative patterns is crucial in the journey towards inner awareness. It requires honesty and courage to acknowledge aspects of ourselves that we might prefer to ignore. Once identified, these patterns can be addressed through various strategies, such as cognitive-behavioral techniques, which help in replacing negative thoughts with more positive and realistic ones. As David D. Burns explains in *Feeling Good: The New Mood Therapy*, '*The way you think about events, not the events themselves, determines the way you feel*'. Embracing this approach allows us to gain control over limiting thoughts and actively reshape our mental landscape toward positivity. Another effective approach is mindfulness meditation, which can increase your awareness of negative thought patterns and enhance your ability to manage them with a non-judgmental attitude. Positive visualization and affirmations are powerful tools in reshaping our inner narrative. By visualizing positive outcomes and repeating affirmations, we can begin to rewrite the script of our subconscious mind, leading to improved self-esteem and a more optimistic outlook on life. These practices encourage a focus on positive aspects of the self and life, fostering a sense of gratitude and abundance.

The journey of developing inner awareness is a deeply personal one, filled with discoveries, challenges, and triumphs. It's a path that requires commitment, patience, and a willingness to embrace vulnerability. By dedicating time to practices such as mindfulness, self-reflection, and positive visualization, you can cultivate a stronger, more resilient sense of self. This inner strength becomes the foundation upon which you can build a life of authenticity, purpose, and joy.

Remember to treat yourself with kindness as you perform these exercises. Gaining inner awareness is about accepting the process of personal development and self-discovery rather than striving for perfection. Celebrate your progress, no matter how small, and recognize that each step forward is a victory in its own right. With each practice, you are not only deepening your understanding of yourself but also enhancing your ability to navigate life with grace, resilience, and empowerment.

What Is Inner Awareness?

Recognizing negative patterns within ourselves can be a daunting task, yet it is a critical component of developing inner awareness. These patterns, often deeply ingrained from past experiences or learned behaviors, can significantly impact our thoughts, emotions, and actions. The first step in addressing these patterns is to identify them through self-reflection and mindfulness. By paying close attention to our reactions and the triggers that cause them, we can begin to see the recurring themes and behaviors that may not be serving our highest good.

Once we have identified these negative patterns, the next step is to actively work on transforming them. This transformation doesn't happen overnight and requires patience, persistence, and a compassionate approach towards oneself. Cognitive-behavioral techniques can be particularly effective in this regard. These strategies involve recognizing distorted thinking and replacing it with more balanced and constructive thoughts. For instance, if you frequently find yourself caught in a cycle of self-doubt, challenge these thoughts by asking for evidence that supports or contradicts this belief. Often, you'll find that your critical inner voice is not an accurate reflection of reality.

Mindfulness meditation is another powerful tool in recognizing and managing negative patterns. By cultivating a practice of mindfulness, you can enhance your ability to observe your thoughts and emotions without judgment. This heightened state of awareness allows you to detach from negative patterns and view them with an objective lens. As you become more adept at noticing your thoughts as they arise, you can gently guide your mind towards more positive and constructive patterns of thinking.

Positive visualization and affirmations are also vital in reshaping our inner narrative. Visualization involves creating a vivid mental image of the outcomes you desire, engaging all your senses to make the experience as real as possible. This technique leverages the brain's neuroplasticity, helping to rewire your thought patterns towards those that support your goals and aspirations. Similarly, affirmations are positive, empowering statements that, when repeated regularly, can help to shift your mindset and self-perception. By affirming your strengths and capabilities, you reinforce your ability to overcome challenges and achieve your goals.

Your path to inner awareness can be greatly impacted by incorporating these practices into your daily routine. It's important to remember that change takes time and that each step forward, no matter how small, is a step towards a more mindful and empowered self. Be gentle with yourself during this process, acknowledging the progress you've made and the resilience you've shown. By committing to this path of self-discovery and growth, you are laying the foundation for a life of authenticity, purpose, and joy.

Mindfulness and Self-Awareness

The cultivation of mindfulness and self-awareness is akin to learning a new language, one that speaks directly to the nuanced experiences of our inner lives. It's a process that invites us to become intimately familiar with the workings of our minds and the rhythms of our emotions, providing a gateway to deeper understanding and connection with ourselves. For those beginning this journey, the concept of mindfulness might seem abstract or elusive, yet its essence is profoundly simple: mindfulness is the practice of being fully present in the moment, aware of our thoughts, feelings, and bodily sensations without judgment or distraction.

To integrate mindfulness into your daily life, start with small, manageable practices. One effective method is to engage in mindful breathing exercises. This can be as simple as taking a few minutes each day to focus solely on your breath, noticing the sensation of air entering and leaving your body, the rise and fall of your chest, and the feeling of aliveness within you. This practice can serve as an anchor, bringing you back to the present moment whenever you find your mind wandering to the past or future.

Another accessible practice is mindful eating, which involves paying close attention to the experience of eating. Notice the colors, textures, and flavors of your food, chewing slowly and appreciating each bite. This not only enhances your enjoyment of the meal but also encourages a more profound gratitude for the nourishment it provides. Similarly, mindful walking— paying close attention to the sensation of your feet touching the ground, the rhythm of your steps, and the air on your skin—can transform a simple activity into a rich, sensory experience.

As you incorporate these practices into your routine, you'll likely notice an increased sense of calm and focus. However, mindfulness is not just about achieving a state of relaxation; it's about developing a deeper awareness of your thought patterns and emotional triggers. This heightened awareness is a powerful tool in recognizing and addressing the negative or self-sabotaging thoughts that can often dominate our inner dialogue.

Self-awareness, closely linked to mindfulness, involves an honest and compassionate examination of our thoughts, feelings, and behaviors. It requires us to observe ourselves with curiosity, without judgment or criticism. This can be challenging, as it involves confronting aspects of ourselves we may find uncomfortable or difficult to accept. Yet, it is through this process of self-reflection that we can begin to understand the root causes of our behaviors and identify the changes we wish to make.

One practical approach to enhancing self-awareness is through journaling. Writing down your thoughts and feelings can help clarify your inner landscape, making it easier to identify patterns and themes in your thoughts and behaviors. Reflecting on your journal entries can provide insight into your emotional triggers and how they influence your reactions and decisions. This practice of self-reflection is not about self-criticism but about gaining a clearer understanding of who you are and how you move through the world.

In developing mindfulness and self-awareness, patience and persistence are key. It's important to approach this process with kindness and compassion towards yourself, recognizing that growth and change are gradual. Celebrate your successes, no matter how small, and view challenges as opportunities for learning and development. Remember, the goal is not to reach a state of perfection but to cultivate a deeper, more compassionate relationship with yourself.

As you deepen your practice of mindfulness and self-awareness, you may find that your relationships with others begin to change as well. By understanding your own thoughts and emotions more clearly, you can approach interactions with more empathy and understanding, fostering deeper connections and more meaningful relationships. This shift not only benefits your personal growth but also enriches the lives of those around you, creating ripples of positive change in your community and beyond.

By dedicating time and effort to these practices, you are taking important steps towards building a life of authenticity, resilience, and fulfillment. The path of mindfulness and self-awareness is one of continuous discovery, offering endless opportunities for growth and transformation. As you go through this course of action, remember that each moment of awareness, each act of self-compassion, is a step towards a more empowered and authentic self.

The Role of Thoughts in Your Life

Our thoughts have an undeniable power to shape our reality, influencing our emotions, behaviors, and ultimately, the outcomes of our lives. This profound impact underscores the importance of cultivating a positive and empowering mindset. By learning to harness the power of our thoughts, we can steer our lives in a direction that aligns with our deepest values and aspirations. The key to this transformation lies in understanding the nature of our thoughts and learning effective strategies to manage them.

The first step in this transformative process is to become acutely aware of the nature of our thoughts. It's crucial to recognize that thoughts are transient and that we have the power to choose which ones we engage with. This realization opens the door to a more empowered state of being, where we are not at the mercy of every passing thought. Instead, we can select thoughts that support our well-being and progress towards our goals.

To effectively manage our thoughts, it's essential to develop a practice of mindfulness. Mindfulness teaches us to observe our thoughts without attachment, allowing them to pass like clouds in the sky. This practice not only helps in reducing stress and anxiety but also empowers us to break free from negative thought patterns that can hinder our growth. By cultivating mindfulness, we enhance our ability to focus on the present moment, appreciating the richness of our experiences without being overshadowed by past regrets or future worries.

Another powerful strategy for shaping our thoughts is the practice of cognitive restructuring. This technique involves identifying negative or unhelpful thoughts and challenging their validity. By questioning the evidence for these thoughts and considering alternative, more positive interpretations, we can gradually shift our mindset towards one that is more optimistic and constructive. Cognitive restructuring is a skill that can be developed with practice, leading to significant improvements in our emotional well-being and resilience.

Affirmations are yet another tool in our arsenal for managing thoughts. These are positive, empowering statements that we repeat to ourselves, designed to counteract negative self-talk and reinforce our self-esteem and confidence. When crafted and used effectively, affirmations can be a powerful means of rewiring our brains towards positivity, helping us to manifest our desired outcomes.

Visualization is a complementary practice that involves creating mental images of the goals we wish to achieve or the person we aspire to be. This technique leverages the brain's remarkable ability to influence our emotions and behaviors through vivid imagery. By regularly visualizing positive outcomes, we prime our minds to recognize and seize opportunities that align with our aspirations.

Incorporating these practices into our daily lives requires commitment and consistency. It's beneficial to set aside specific times each day for mindfulness meditation, cognitive restructuring exercises, affirmations, and visualization. These practices can be integrated into our routines, such as during morning rituals or evening reflections, making them a natural part of our journey towards self-improvement.

It's also important to cultivate an environment that supports positive thinking. This can involve surrounding ourselves with people who uplift and inspire us, consuming content that enriches our minds, and engaging in activities that nourish our souls. As James Clear notes in Atomic Habits, *'You do not rise to the level of your goals; you fall to the level of your systems'*. By intentionally creating a supportive ecosystem around us—a 'system' of positive influences and habits—we make it easier to maintain a resilient and optimistic mindset, even when faced with challenges. Just as our environment can hinder us, it can also empower us to stay focused, grounded, and aligned with our aspirations. Cultivating this supportive environment becomes an essential part of our journey toward a life of purpose and fulfillment.

On this path of managing our thoughts, it's crucial to approach ourselves with compassion and patience.

Change is a gradual process, and there will be moments of setback. During these times, it's important to remind ourselves of our progress and the power we have to shape our thoughts and, by extension, our lives. By persisting in our efforts and embracing the journey of self-discovery, we unlock the potential to transform our lives in profound ways, achieving a state of inner strength and fulfillment that radiates outward, touching every aspect of our existence.

Exercise n.1: Thought Journal

Objective: Get awareness of thought patterns and their impact on mood.

Duration: Daily, for at least 2 weeks.

Instructions:

1. <u>Daily Reflection (10-15 minutes):</u>
   - *Identify Thoughts*: Write down significant thoughts from the day. (ex. "I'm not good enough for this project")
   - *Context:* Describe the situation when these thoughts occurred. (ex. During a meeting)
   - *Emotional Impact:* Note how these thoughts made you feel. (ex. Felt anxious)
   - *Behavioral Response:* Record any actions resulting from these thoughts. (ex. Procrastinated)
   - *Mindfulness Check:* Observe your thoughts without judgment. (ex. Recurring work-related stress)
   - *Cognitive Restructuring:* Challenge negative thoughts and find positive alternatives. (ex. "I've completed similar projects before")
   - *Affirmations*: Write and repeat a positive affirmation. (ex. "I'm capable and competent")
   - *Visualization*: Visualize a positive outcome or goal. (Visualized completing the project successfully)

2. <u>Weekly Reflection:</u>
   Review entries, note patterns, and summarize progress.

3. <u>Supportive Environment:</u>
   Surround yourself with positive influences and activities.

4. <u>Self-Compassion:</u>
   Be kind and patient with yourself throughout the process.

Daily Mindfulness Practices

Observing thoughts without judgment is a pivotal practice in cultivating daily mindfulness. This technique encourages individuals to become aware of their thoughts as they arise, without immediately categorizing them as good or bad, right or wrong. It's about creating a space where thoughts can be acknowledged and then gently set aside, allowing for a moment of peace amidst the chaos of daily life. By practicing this form of non-judgmental observation, you can begin to break the cycle of automatic reactions to thoughts and feelings, fostering a deeper sense of inner calm and awareness.

Another essential practice is engaging in **mindful breathing**. This can be as simple as taking a few minutes each day to focus solely on your breath. Sit in a comfortable position, close your eyes, and take deep, slow breaths. Inhale through your nose, feeling your chest and belly rise, and exhale through your mouth, feeling a sense of release. Mindful breathing serves as an anchor, bringing you back to the present moment and reducing stress and anxiety.

Incorporating **body scans** into your routine can also enhance mindfulness. This involves lying down or sitting comfortably and paying attention to different parts of your body in turn, from your toes to your head. Notice any sensations, tension, or discomfort without trying to change anything. This practice can lead to a profound connection between mind and body, highlighting areas of stress and promoting relaxation.

Mindful walking is another practice that can be easily added to daily routines. Instead of walking with the aim of getting from one place to another, mindful walking focuses on the experience of walking itself. Pay attention to the sensation of your feet touching the ground, the rhythm of your steps, and the movement of your body. This practice can transform a simple act into a meditative experience, fostering a deep appreciation for the present moment.

Lastly, **eating mindfully** is a practice that not only enhances your relationship with food but also with yourself. It involves paying full attention to the experience of eating, from the flavors and textures of the food to the sensations of fullness and satisfaction. Eating mindfully can help break the cycle of mindless eating and promote a healthier, more joyful relationship with food.

By integrating these practices into your daily life, you can cultivate a deeper sense of mindfulness and awareness, laying the foundation for a more present, peaceful, and fulfilling life.

Morning Thought Journaling

Building on the foundation of mindfulness and self-awareness practices, morning thought journaling emerges as a powerful tool to deepen your inner awareness and start your day with intention. This practice involves dedicating a few moments each morning to write down your thoughts, feelings, and intentions for the day. The act of putting pen to paper right after waking up captures the raw, unfiltered essence of your thoughts, which is often lost as the day progresses and external demands take over. It's not about crafting perfectly structured sentences but allowing a stream of consciousness to flow, revealing insights into your inner state, desires, and areas that may need attention.

To incorporate morning thought journaling into your daily routine, consider keeping a journal and pen beside your bed, making it the first thing you reach for upon waking. Start by writing down three things you're grateful for, which primes your mind to look for the positive rather than dwelling on the negatives. Then, jot down any dreams you can recall, as dreams can be a window into your subconscious, offering clues to your inner desires and fears. Follow this with a free write section where you let your thoughts wander without judgment, exploring how you feel, what's weighing on your mind, and what you're looking forward to. Conclude your journaling by setting an intention for the day—a focus or mindset you wish to maintain, an action you aim to accomplish, or a quality you want to embody.

The beauty of morning thought journaling lies in its simplicity and the personal insights it can unlock. It serves as a daily check-in with yourself, fostering a habit of introspection and mindfulness that strengthens your inner awareness. Over time, reviewing your journal entries can reveal patterns in your thoughts and behaviors, highlighting areas of growth and aspects of your life that may require change. By making morning thought journaling a non-negotiable part of your routine, you set a tone of self-care and intentionality that carries through the rest of your day, contributing significantly to your journey of cultivating a happier, more mindful, and authentic life.

Exercise n.2: Morning Thought Journaling

Objective: Enhance inner awareness and start your day with intention.
Duration: Daily, each morning.
Instructions:

1. Preparation:
   Keep a journal and pen beside your bed to reach for immediately upon waking.

2. Daily Reflection (5-10 minutes):
   - *Gratitude:* Write down three things you're grateful for. (ex. Grateful for the supportive family, for good health, for the opportunity to learn new things)
   - *Dream Recall:* Note any dreams you remember. (ex. Dreamt about walking through a serene forest, feeling peaceful)
   - *Free Write:* Allow your thoughts to flow without judgment. Explore your feelings, what's on your mind, and what you're looking forward to. (ex. Feeling a bit anxious about the upcoming meeting. Looking forward to spending time with friends in the evening. Noticed a recurring thought about needing more balance in life.)
   - *Set an Intention:* Define a focus or mindset for the day, an action to accomplish, or a quality to embody. (ex. Intend to stay calm and focused during the meeting. Aim to listen actively and contribute positively.)

3. Weekly Review:
   Reflect on your entries to identify patterns in your thoughts and behaviors. Note areas of growth and aspects needing change. (ex. Noticed recurring themes of seeking balance and feeling anxious about work. Progress made in setting daily intentions and recognizing areas for personal growth.)

4. Consistency:
   Make this journaling practice a non-negotiable part of your morning routine to foster self-care and intentionality

Observing Thoughts Without Judgment

Transitioning from the foundational practices of mindfulness and morning thought journaling, we delve deeper into the essence of observing thoughts without judgment, a critical skill for fostering inner awareness and tranquility. This practice is not merely about recognizing the presence of thoughts but about cultivating an attitude of curiosity and openness towards them. It's about learning to see thoughts as transient events in the mind, much like clouds passing in the sky, without attaching ourselves to them or letting them dictate our emotional state.

The key to mastering this skill lies in the consistent application of gentle awareness. When you notice your mind wandering or getting caught up in specific thoughts, gently acknowledge this without criticism and guide your focus back to the present moment, perhaps by concentrating on your breath or the sensations in your body. This act of returning your attention to the now, time and again, strengthens your ability to remain centered and calm, even amidst the hustle and bustle of daily life.

To enhance your practice, it might be helpful to visualize your thoughts as leaves floating down a stream. Observe each leaf as it passes by without attempting to alter its course. Some leaves may move slowly, while others rush by; similarly, some thoughts may linger, while others swiftly pass. The objective is not to empty the mind of thoughts but to observe their natural flow without entanglement or judgment.

Another effective approach is to label your thoughts neutrally as they arise. For instance, you might note a thought as "planning," "remembering," or "worrying." This simple act of labeling creates a buffer between you and your thoughts, providing you with the space to choose how, or if, you'll engage with them. Over time, this practice can lead to a profound shift in how you relate to your thoughts and emotions, moving from a place of reactivity to one of mindful response.

Integrating the practice of observing thoughts without judgment into your daily life requires patience and persistence. It's a skill that develops gradually, through regular practice. You may find it beneficial to dedicate specific times of the day for mindfulness practice, such as during your morning routine or in the evening before bed. However, the true power of this practice is realized when it becomes an integral part of your day-to-day activities, allowing you to remain present and centered no matter what life throws your way.

By cultivating the ability to observe your thoughts without judgment, you empower yourself to navigate life's challenges with greater ease and resilience. This practice fosters a deeper connection to your inner self, enabling you to live more authentically and with a sense of peace. As you continue to explore and deepen your mindfulness practices, remember that each moment offers a new opportunity for growth and self-discovery. Through consistent practice and gentle self-compassion, you can transform your relationship with your thoughts and emotions, paving the way for a more mindful, empowered, and fulfilling life.

Exercise n.3: Non-Judgmental Thought Observation

Objective: Practice non-judgmental observation to detach from temporary emotions. This is a Mindfulness Practice.
Duration: Daily, for at least 10 minutes.

Instructions:

Find a Quiet Space:
Choose a calm and comfortable place where you won't be disturbed.

Set a Timer:
Set a timer for 10 minutes to ensure you dedicate the full time to the practice.

Focus on Your Breath:
Begin by taking a few deep breaths to center yourself. Focus on the sensation of your breath entering and leaving your body.

Observe Your Thoughts:
- As thoughts arise, simply observe them without judgment. Imagine each thought as a cloud passing by in the sky.
- Avoid labeling thoughts as "good" or "bad." Just note their presence and let them pass.

Detach from Emotions:
- Notice any emotions that accompany your thoughts. Recognize that these emotions are temporary and do not define you.
- Allow yourself to feel the emotion without trying to change it. Acknowledge its presence and let it pass naturally.

Return to Your Breath:
Whenever you find yourself getting caught up in a thought or emotion, gently bring your focus back to your breath.

End with Gratitude:
When the timer goes off, take a moment to express gratitude for the time you've dedicated to this practice.

Daily Reflection:
After the session, jot down any observations or insights in a journal. Note any recurring thoughts or emotions and your reactions to them.

Building a Foundation of Self-Reflection

Self-reflection is the cornerstone of personal growth and inner awareness. It involves taking a step back to evaluate your thoughts, feelings, behaviors, and overall life experiences. This process allows for a deeper understanding of oneself, fostering growth and change where necessary. To build a strong foundation of self-reflection, it's crucial to establish a routine that encourages regular introspection.

One effective method is to set aside a designated time each day for reflection. This could be in the morning as you plan your day or in the evening as you wind down. Use this time to ponder the events of the day, your reactions to them, and how they align with your core values and goals. Consider the emotions you experienced, why you felt them, and how you can manage them more effectively in the future.

Journaling is another powerful tool for self-reflection. It provides a tangible way to track your thoughts, feelings, and the decisions you make over time. By regularly writing down your experiences, you can identify patterns in your behavior and thought processes that you may want to change. Additionally, journaling can serve as a therapeutic outlet for expressing feelings that might be difficult to articulate verbally.

Asking for feedback from trusted friends or family members can also enhance your self-reflective practice. Sometimes, an outside perspective can offer insight into aspects of ourselves that we might overlook or be unaware of. Be open to receiving constructive criticism and use it as a basis for reflection and growth.

Practicing mindfulness is another key aspect of building a foundation of self-reflection. Mindfulness involves being fully present and engaged in the moment without judgment. By cultivating mindfulness, you can become more aware of your thoughts and feelings as they occur, allowing for immediate reflection on your reactions and behaviors.

Finally, setting personal goals and regularly reviewing them is an essential part of self-reflection. Goals give you direction and purpose and reviewing them allows you to assess your progress and make adjustments as needed. This practice ensures that your actions are aligned with your values and long-term objectives, fostering a sense of accomplishment and satisfaction.

By incorporating these practices into your daily routine, you can develop a robust foundation of self-reflection. This foundation will enable you to live more intentionally, make more informed decisions, and ultimately lead a more fulfilling and authentic life. Remember, the goal of self-reflection is not to be overly critical of oneself but to foster growth, understanding, and compassion for oneself and others.

Recognizing Negative Patterns

Recognizing negative patterns in our thoughts and behaviors is a pivotal step towards fostering a more mindful and intentional life. These patterns, often deeply ingrained from past experiences or learned behaviors, can significantly hinder our personal growth and inner peace. The key to breaking free from these detrimental cycles lies in our ability to identify and understand them, thereby empowering us to initiate positive change.

The first step in this transformative process is to develop a heightened sense of self-awareness. By becoming more attuned to our thoughts, emotions, and reactions, we can start to pinpoint the recurring themes that may be contributing to our dissatisfaction or distress. For instance, you might notice a tendency to engage in self-critical thoughts when faced with a challenge, or a pattern of procrastination when it comes to pursuing your goals. These observations are crucial, as they lay the groundwork for the introspective work that follows.

Once these patterns have been identified, the next phase involves delving deeper to understand their origins and the needs they are attempting to fulfill. Often, negative patterns are protective mechanisms that served a purpose at one point in our lives but have since become maladaptive. By uncovering the underlying beliefs and fears driving these behaviors, we can begin to address them with compassion and understanding. For example, a pattern of avoiding conflict may stem from a fear of rejection or a belief that one's needs are not important. Recognizing this allows for the exploration of healthier ways to communicate and assert oneself.

The process of transforming negative patterns into positive behaviors requires patience, persistence, and a willingness to experiment with new approaches. Start small by choosing one pattern you wish to change and brainstorming alternative actions or thoughts that align more closely with the person you aspire to be. If self-criticism is a persistent issue, try implementing a practice of daily affirmations that reinforce your worth and capabilities. Alternatively, if procrastination is the pattern you're tackling, break your goals into smaller, manageable tasks and celebrate each accomplishment, no matter how minor it may seem.

Accountability plays a crucial role in this journey. Sharing your goals and challenges with a trusted friend, family member, or therapist can provide you with the support and encouragement needed to stay on track. Additionally, keeping a journal of your progress can be incredibly rewarding, offering tangible evidence of the strides you're making towards breaking free from negative patterns and cultivating a more empowered and authentic life.

It's important to approach this process with kindness and refrain from self-judgment. Change is inherently challenging, and setbacks are a natural part of growth. When you find yourself reverting to old patterns, view it as an opportunity to learn and refine your strategies rather than a failure. With each attempt, you'll gain deeper insights into yourself and develop stronger resilience, ultimately leading to lasting transformation.

By dedicating yourself to recognizing and transforming negative patterns, you embark on a path towards greater self-awareness, fulfillment, and inner strength. This commitment to personal evolution not only enhances your own life but also enriches your relationships with others, contributing to a more mindful and compassionate world. Embrace this endeavor with an open heart and mind and watch as your life unfolds in more meaningful and vibrant ways.

Exercise n.4: Identifying Negative Patterns Exercise

Objective: Recognize and interrupt recurring negative patterns.
Type: Reflection and Awareness Exercise
Duration: Daily, for at least 2 weeks.

Instructions:
Set Aside Time: Dedicate 10-15 minutes each day. Consistency is key.

Create Your Journal Entry: Use a notebook, digital document, or journaling app.

Daily Reflection Prompts:
- *Identify Negative Thoughts*: Write down specific negative thoughts and when they occurred.
- *Context and Triggers*: Describe the situation, people, and events surrounding these thoughts.
- *Emotional Impact*: Reflect on the emotions these thoughts evoked (e.g., sadness, anger, anxiety).
- *Behavioral Response*: Note any actions or behaviors resulting from these thoughts.
- *Pattern Recognition*: Look for recurring themes or triggers.
- *Interrupting the Cycle*: Consider alternative thoughts or actions to break the cycle.

Weekly Review: Review your entries at the end of each week. Summarize patterns and progress in interrupting negative cycles.

Supportive Environment: Note any changes in your environment that support positive thinking (e.g., spending time with uplifting people, consuming positive content).

Self-Compassion: Be kind and patient with yourself. Acknowledge your efforts and remember that change is gradual.

Positive Visualization and Affirmations

Harnessing the power of positive visualization and affirmations can significantly amplify your journey of self-discovery and inner strength development. This transformative practice involves envisioning your best self and your desired outcomes, coupled with the repetition of empowering statements that reinforce your ability to achieve them. The synergy of visualization and affirmations acts as a catalyst for change, embedding a deep-seated belief in your capabilities and potential.

Positive visualization starts with creating a vivid mental image of achieving your goals and embodying the qualities you aspire to possess. For example, if you're working toward a promotion, picture yourself confidently delivering a successful presentation, feeling the satisfaction of recognition and respect from your colleagues. Or if you aspire to improve your fitness, see yourself crossing the finish line of a race, feeling strong and accomplished. Imagine navigating challenges with grace and resilience, engaging in meaningful relationships, and living in alignment with your core values. For instance, if you wish to deepen your relationships, visualize yourself listening attentively to a loved one, feeling connected and valued in their presence. The key is to engage all your senses in the visualization process, making the experience as real and detailed as possible. Feel the emotions you would experience upon achieving your goals, hear the words of affirmation and support from those around you, and see yourself thriving in your envisioned scenario.

Affirmations, on the other hand, are positive, present-tense statements that you repeat to yourself, designed to challenge and undermine negative beliefs and replace them with constructive, empowering thoughts. For instance, if self-doubt often holds you back, try saying, "I am fully capable of handling any challenge that comes my way." If you struggle with self-worth, use an affirmation like, "I deserve love and respect," or, to boost motivation, "I have the power to create meaningful change in my life." Crafting effective affirmations involves focusing on your strengths, achievements, and the positive attributes you wish to cultivate. These statements reinforce your self-belief and motivation, gradually shifting your mindset from one of limitation to one of possibility and empowerment.

Integrating positive visualization and affirmations into your daily routine requires consistency and intentionality. Dedicate a few minutes each day, preferably in the morning or before bed, to close your eyes and visualize your desired future while repeating your affirmations aloud or in your mind. For instance, you might start your day by visualizing a productive and fulfilling day ahead, affirming, "Today, I approach every task with focus and energy." This practice not only sets a positive tone for your day but also embeds these empowering beliefs into your subconscious, gradually aligning your mindset and behaviors with your aspirations.

To enhance the effectiveness of this practice, consider creating a vision board that represents your goals and dreams through images and words. For example, if financial security is a goal, place images of financial success or stability on your board. If health is a priority, include images that evoke vitality and strength. Place the board somewhere you will see it every day as a visual reminder of what you are working toward. Additionally, recording your affirmations and listening to them during moments of downtime can reinforce their impact, making it easier for you to internalize these positive messages.

Remember, the goal of positive visualization and affirmations is not to deny the reality of challenges or difficulties but to equip you with the mindset and confidence needed to navigate them successfully. By focusing on positive outcomes and reinforcing your self-worth and capabilities, you create a fertile ground for growth, resilience, and fulfillment. Visualize yourself handling a future obstacle with calm and control, reinforcing with an affirmation like, "I face challenges with courage and resilience." As you practice visualizing your achievements and affirming your potential, you'll find that your actions and decisions begin to align more closely with your vision of success, propelling you forward on your path to a more mindful, empowered, and authentic life.

Exercise n.5: Positive Visualization and Affirmation Practice

Objective: Promote positive thinking and affirmation through morning visualization.

Type: Visualization and Affirmation

Duration: Daily, each morning.

Instructions:

Set Aside Time: Dedicate 5-10 minutes each morning.

Find a Quiet Space: Choose a calm and comfortable place.

Daily Practice:
- *Relax and Center Yourself*: Sit comfortably, close your eyes, and take a few deep breaths.
- *Positive Visualization*: Visualize a positive outcome or goal in vivid detail. Imagine the emotions you would feel upon achieving it.
- *Create Affirmations*: Craft a few positive affirmations that align with your visualization. Examples: "I am capable and confident." "I attract positive opportunities." "I am worthy of success."
- *Repeat Affirmations*: Repeat your affirmations with conviction, at least three times.
- *Anchor the Positive Feelings*: Feel the emotions of success and confidence in your body.

Daily Reflection: After the practice, jot down any observations or feelings in a journal.

Weekly Review: At the end of each week, review your journal entries and reflect on your progress.

Consistency: Make this practice a non-negotiable part of your morning routine.

Core Values and Purpose

I dentifying your core values and purpose is akin to laying the foundation for a house that embodies your true self. It's about discovering what truly matters to you, beyond societal expectations or external influences. This process is deeply personal and requires introspection and honesty. Your core values are the guiding principles that dictate behavior and action; they help you understand what is fundamentally important in your life. Purpose, on the other hand, gives your life direction and adds meaning to the things you do and the choices you make.

To start this journey, begin by reflecting on moments in your life when you felt truly happy, fulfilled, or proud. Ask yourself what these moments have in common. Perhaps you'll find that connection, creativity, or learning stands out. These are clues to your core values. Additionally, think about times when you were most unhappy or frustrated. Often, these feelings stem from living in ways that contradict your values. Recognizing these patterns is crucial in understanding what your core values are not.

Another effective method is to consider the qualities you admire in others. Sometimes, what we respect in other people reflects the values we aspire to embody. Make a list of people you admire and the qualities they possess that resonate with you. This exercise can offer insights into values that you may wish to adopt or strengthen in your own life.

Purpose can be more elusive, as it involves understanding why you do what you do and what you wish to achieve in the broader scheme of your life. It's about looking beyond daily tasks and considering the legacy you want to leave. To uncover your purpose, ask yourself what you're passionate about and how you can use those passions to serve others or contribute to a larger cause. Think about the issues that stir you emotionally or the problems you're naturally drawn to solving.

Remember, identifying your core values and purpose is not a one-time task but an ongoing process. As you grow and evolve, so too might your values and sense of purpose. Be open to this evolution and allow yourself the flexibility to adapt. The key is to remain authentic to yourself at each stage of your life, ensuring that your actions and decisions align with your deepest beliefs and aspirations.

Engaging in this reflective process can be transformative. It not only brings clarity to your decision-making but also enhances your overall sense of well-being. By understanding and honoring your core values and purpose, you forge a path that is uniquely yours, one that leads to greater fulfillment and happiness.

Once you have begun to identify your core values and purpose, the next step involves integrating them into your daily life. This means making conscious choices that are in harmony with your values and moving steadily towards your purpose. Start by evaluating your current habits and routines. Ask yourself whether these practices support or detract from your core values. If you find discrepancies, it's time to consider making changes. For instance, if one of your core values is health, yet your daily routine lacks any form of physical activity, introducing a simple exercise regimen could be a beneficial alignment.

Moreover, setting goals that reflect your values and purpose can significantly enhance your sense of fulfillment. These goals don't have to be monumental; even small, achievable objectives can lead to profound satisfaction. For example, if lifelong learning is a value you cherish, setting a goal to read one new book each month aligns with this value and contributes to your personal growth.

Incorporating your values into your decision-making process is also crucial. Before making decisions, big or small, consider how each option aligns with your core values. This approach ensures that your choices are more deliberate and meaningful, reducing the likelihood of regret and increasing your overall happiness.

Additionally, sharing your journey of discovering and living by your core values can deepen your connections with others. Authentic conversations about values and purpose can foster more meaningful relationships. These discussions can also provide new insights and perspectives, further enriching your understanding of your own values and purpose.

Remember, living in alignment with your core values and purpose is not about perfection. It's about making more choices that reflect what's truly important to you, learning from the experiences that don't align with your values, and continually striving to lead a life that feels authentic and fulfilling. As you practice this alignment, you'll likely notice a stronger sense of self, increased confidence, and a deeper connection to the world around you.

Finally, consider keeping a journal to document your reflections and progress. Journaling about your experiences, the challenges you face, and the victories you achieve can provide valuable insights into your personal growth. It can also serve as a reminder of your resilience and ability to adapt your values and purpose as you navigate through life.

By engaging in these practices, you not only honor your core values and purpose but also empower yourself to lead a life of greater intention, satisfaction, and joy.

Uncovering Your Core Values

As you delve into the process of **uncovering your core values**, it becomes essential to engage in activities that prompt deeper self-exploration. One effective method is to **create a vision board** that represents your ideals, aspirations, and what you stand for. This visual representation can serve as a daily reminder of your core values and motivate you to align your actions accordingly. Gather magazines, photographs, quotes, and any other items that resonate with you. As you select these elements, pay attention to the themes that emerge. These themes are indicative of your values and can guide you in making life choices that are in harmony with your true self.

Another powerful exercise is to **write a personal mission statement**. This statement should encapsulate your core values, how you intend to apply them in your life, and the impact you wish to have on the world. Begin by reflecting on questions such as, "What qualities do I admire in others and wish to embody?" and "How can I contribute to my community in a way that is meaningful to me?" Crafting this statement can clarify your purpose and offer a guiding light as you navigate life's challenges and opportunities.

Engaging in regular self-reflection is also crucial. Dedicate time each week to journal about your experiences, focusing on moments when you felt your actions were fully aligned with your values, as well as times when you felt off course. This practice can highlight areas for growth and help you make more conscious choices moving forward.

Seek feedback from trusted friends and family about what they perceive your values to be. Often, those close to us can offer insights into our character that we may overlook. Engage in open and honest conversations about how they see your values manifesting in your behavior and decisions. This external perspective can be invaluable in affirming or refining your understanding of your core values.

Finally, **commit to lifelong learning** about values and ethics. Read books, attend workshops, and participate in discussions that challenge and expand your perspective on what it means to live a value-driven life. This commitment to growth ensures that your understanding of your core values evolves as you do, allowing for a dynamic and authentic expression of your true self.

By incorporating these practices into your life, you actively participate in the ongoing journey of self-discovery. This journey is not always linear or easy, but it is deeply rewarding. Through intentional reflection and action, you can ensure that your life is a true reflection of your core values, leading to a more fulfilling and authentic existence.

Why Values Matter in Everyday Life

Living in alignment with one's core values profoundly influences every aspect of daily life, from the decisions we make to the relationships we nurture and the personal goals we set. When values are clear, making choices becomes easier and more straightforward, as each decision can be weighed against these guiding principles. This alignment ensures that the life one leads is not only fulfilling but also authentic and true to one's inner self. For individuals embarking on the path of personal growth and seeking to forge inner strength, understanding the pivotal role of values in everyday life is essential.

Values serve as a compass, directing behavior in a way that is congruent with one's deepest beliefs and convictions. This congruence fosters a sense of integrity and wholeness, as actions and thoughts are consistently aligned with personal truth. For example, if one values family above all, prioritizing time with loved ones becomes a non-negotiable aspect of daily life. Similarly, if one holds honesty in high regard, this value will dictate how one communicates and interacts with others, ensuring relationships are built on trust and transparency.

Moreover, recognizing and living by one's values can significantly enhance resilience in the face of adversity. When challenges arise, as they inevitably do, values act as a sturdy foundation upon which one can stand firm. They provide a source of motivation and encouragement, reminding individuals of what is truly important and why perseverance is worthwhile. This resilience is further bolstered by the congruence between values and actions, which contributes to a strong sense of self-efficacy and confidence.

In addition to guiding personal choices and fostering resilience, values play a crucial role in the cultivation of meaningful relationships. Authentic connections are formed on the basis of shared values and mutual respect for each other's guiding principles. When values align, relationships are enriched with a deeper understanding and appreciation for one another, paving the way for genuine, lasting bonds. Conversely, awareness of differing values can aid in navigating relationships more mindfully, respecting boundaries and embracing diversity without compromising one's own values.

Values also influence goal setting and personal development. Goals that are rooted in one's core values are imbued with personal significance, making them more compelling and motivating. This alignment ensures that the pursuit of these goals is not only rewarding but also contributes to a greater sense of purpose and fulfillment. Whether the goal is to advance in one's career, improve physical health, or contribute to the community, grounding these aspirations in core values amplifies their impact and relevance.

In the realm of personal growth and self-improvement, the importance of values cannot be overstated. They are the essence of who one is and aspire to be, shaping not only individual identity but also the mark one leaves on the world. By making values a central aspect of daily life, individuals empower themselves to lead lives of authenticity, purpose, and profound satisfaction. This empowerment is a testament to the transformative power of living in alignment with one's core values, a cornerstone of forging inner strength and achieving lifelong empowerment.

Exercise n.6: Values Visualization Exercise

Objective: Identify core values and link them to personal actions.
Type: Self-Discovery Exercise
Duration: Daily, for at least 10 minutes.

Instructions:
Set Aside Time: Dedicate 10 minutes each day.

Find a Quiet Space: Choose a calm and comfortable place.

Daily Practice:
- *Relax and Center Yourself*: Sit comfortably, close your eyes, and take a few deep breaths.
- *Identify Core Values*: Reflect on what is most important to you in life. Write down 3-5 core values (e.g., honesty, kindness, growth).
- *Visualize Living Your Values*: Visualize a day where you fully live according to your core values. Imagine specific actions and interactions.
- *Link Values to Actions*: Identify specific actions you can take today to align with each core value. Write these actions down.
- *Set an Intention*: Commit to incorporating these value-driven actions into your day.

Daily Reflection: At the end of the day, reflect on how well you lived according to your values. Note any actions you took and their impact.

Weekly Review: At the end of each week, review your journal entries. Reflect on patterns and progress.

Consistency: Make this exercise a non-negotiable part of your daily routine.

Setting Goals with Your Values

When it comes to **setting goals aligned with your values**, the first step is to ensure that each goal you set reflects what truly matters to you. This alignment is crucial for not only achieving the goal but also for maintaining motivation and satisfaction throughout the journey. To start, consider your identified core values and how they can translate into specific, actionable goals. For instance, if one of your core values is **compassion**, you might set a goal to volunteer a certain number of hours each month at a local charity. This direct alignment ensures that your actions reinforce and reflect your values, providing a sense of fulfillment and purpose.

Break down your goals into manageable steps. Large, ambitious goals can often feel overwhelming, leading to procrastination or a sense of failure. By breaking down each goal into smaller, actionable steps, you make the goal more attainable and less daunting. For example, if your goal is to run a marathon and fitness is a core value, start with shorter runs and gradually increase your distance. This method not only helps in achieving the goal but also aligns with the value of **self-improvement** and **perseverance**.

Set SMART goals - Specific, Measurable, Achievable, Relevant, and Time-bound. This framework ensures that your goals are well-defined and trackable, making it easier to gauge progress and stay motivated. For instance, rather than setting a vague goal like "get fit," a SMART goal would be "attend three fitness classes per week for the next three months." This specificity ensures that the goal is in direct alignment with your value of

health and is structured in a way that fosters accountability and progress.

Reflect on your progress regularly. Regular reflection allows you to assess whether your actions are still in alignment with your values and goals. It also provides an opportunity to adjust your goals as needed. Life is dynamic, and your goals should be flexible enough to accommodate growth and change. If you find that a certain goal no longer aligns with your core values or the direction you wish to take, don't hesitate to revise it. This adaptability is key to ensuring that your goals continue to reflect your true self.

Celebrate your achievements, no matter how small. Achieving goals that are aligned with your core values is a significant accomplishment and should be recognized. Celebrating these achievements reinforces positive behavior and motivates you to continue pursuing your values-driven goals. Whether it's treating yourself to a nice meal or simply taking a moment to reflect on your journey, acknowledging your success is crucial.

Incorporate accountability by sharing your goals with someone who understands and supports your values. This could be a friend, family member, or mentor. Having someone to share your progress with can provide additional motivation and encouragement. It also offers an external perspective that can be invaluable in overcoming obstacles and staying on track.

Remember, the goal of setting values-aligned goals is not just to achieve specific outcomes but to lead a life that is consistent with your deepest beliefs and aspirations. By following these steps, you not only move closer to achieving your goals but also ensure that the path you take is fulfilling, authentic, and true to who you are.

Short-Term vs. Long-Term Goals

Distinguishing between short-term and long-term goals is essential for anyone striving to lead a life that resonates with their core values and purpose. Short-term goals, typically set to be achieved within a few weeks to a year, serve as stepping stones towards the broader, more ambitious long-term goals that can span several years or even a lifetime. The beauty of setting both types of goals lies in their ability to create a roadmap for a life lived with intention and fulfillment.

When aligning goals with your values, it's crucial to start by setting short-term goals that not only reflect but also reinforce your core values. These goals are more immediate and often easier to accomplish, providing a sense of progress and motivation as you work towards the more significant, long-term aspirations. For instance, if one of your core values is health, a short-term goal might be to incorporate a 30-minute walk into your daily routine. This simple, achievable aim supports your value of health and sets the foundation for more ambitious goals, like running a half-marathon.

On the other hand, long-term goals require patience, persistence, and a deep connection to your core values. They are the ultimate expression of what you hope to achieve in life, often encompassing personal, professional, and spiritual aspirations. These goals are more complex and challenging, demanding a higher level of commitment and resilience. Continuing with the health example, a long-term goal could be to maintain a healthy lifestyle that allows you to engage in physical activities well into your later years, embodying a lifelong commitment to your value of health.

The interplay between short-term and long-term goals is dynamic. Achieving short-term goals provides the momentum and confidence needed to tackle the more daunting long-term ones. Each small victory is a building block, reinforcing your belief in your ability to achieve greater things. This incremental approach ensures that your journey towards living in alignment with your core values is filled with continuous learning, growth, and satisfaction.

To effectively set and pursue these goals, consider employing specific strategies such as writing them down in a place where you'll see them daily, thus keeping them at the forefront of your mind. Additionally, regularly review and adjust your goals to reflect any changes in your values, circumstances, or insights gained along the way. This flexibility is key to staying aligned with your core values as you evolve over time.

Moreover, it's beneficial to share your goals with a supportive community or mentor who can offer encouragement, hold you accountable, and celebrate your successes with you. This external support can be invaluable, especially when facing obstacles or when motivation wanes.

Incorporating both short-term and long-term goals into your life strategy allows for a balanced approach to personal development. It ensures that you are making consistent progress towards your ultimate aspirations while also celebrating the smaller achievements along the way. This dual focus not only enriches your journey but also deepens your connection to your core values, guiding you towards a life of purpose, fulfillment, and true inner strength.

Remember, the essence of setting goals aligned with your values is not merely in the achievement of these goals but in the journey itself—the daily practices, decisions, and reflections that shape who you are and who you aspire to be. Through this mindful approach to goal setting, you empower yourself to navigate life with intention, resilience, and authenticity, creating a legacy that reflects your deepest values and highest aspirations.

Aligning Actions with Values

Aligning actions with values is the cornerstone of living a life that is not only meaningful but also deeply satisfying. When your daily actions reflect your core values, you create a harmonious existence that resonates with your true self, leading to an enhanced sense of fulfillment and happiness. This alignment is crucial for anyone seeking to develop inner strength and navigate life with intention and purpose. To achieve this, it's important to take practical steps that bridge the gap between understanding your values and living them out through your actions.

One effective strategy is to conduct a regular audit of your life to ensure your actions are in alignment with your values. This involves examining various aspects of your life, such as your career, relationships, and personal habits, and assessing whether they reflect your core values. For instance, if one of your core values is creativity, but you find yourself in a job that stifles this, it might be time to explore new opportunities that allow you to express your creativity more freely. Similarly, if you value community but have been isolating yourself, seeking out group activities or volunteering could realign your actions with your values.

Creating a value-action plan can also be incredibly beneficial. This plan outlines specific, actionable steps you can take to live according to your values. For example, if you value health, your plan might include actions like scheduling regular exercise, preparing healthy meals, or setting a bedtime to ensure adequate rest. This plan acts as a roadmap, guiding your daily choices and helping you to stay focused on what truly matters to you.

Another key aspect of aligning actions with values is setting boundaries. Boundaries allow you to protect your time and energy, ensuring that you can focus on activities that align with your values. They also help you to say no to things that detract from your values, creating space for what enriches your life. For example, if you value family time, setting boundaries around work hours can help ensure that you're able to dedicate time to your loved ones.

It's also essential to surround yourself with people who share or respect your values. Relationships play a significant role in our lives, and being around like-minded individuals can reinforce your commitment to living according to your values. These individuals can offer support, motivation, and accountability, making it easier for you to stay aligned with your values in your actions.

Practicing mindfulness is another powerful tool for aligning actions with values. By staying present and aware, you can make more conscious choices that reflect your values. Mindfulness helps you recognize when your actions are drifting away from your values and provides the clarity needed to adjust your course. This could be as simple as taking a moment to breathe and center yourself before making a decision, ensuring that your choices are deliberate and aligned with your core values.

Finally, embracing flexibility and forgiveness is crucial in the process of aligning actions with values. There will be times when you falter, and your actions may not perfectly align with your values. In these moments, it's important to practice self-compassion, learn from the experience, and gently realign your actions with your values. Growth and learning are integral parts of this journey, and accepting them can make the process of aligning actions with values a fulfilling and enriching experience.

By taking these practical steps, you actively bridge the gap between understanding your values and living them out through your actions. This alignment is a dynamic and ongoing process, one that requires attention, intention, and a willingness to grow. Through consistent effort and reflection, you can ensure that your life is a true reflection of your core values, leading to greater satisfaction, happiness, and inner strength.

Exercise n.7: Value-Aligned Goal Setting Exercise

Objective: Set goals that reflect personal values for consistency and fulfillment.
Type: Goal-Setting Exercise
Duration: Daily, for at least 10 minutes.

Instructions:
Set Aside Time: Dedicate 10 minutes each day.

Find a Quiet Space: Choose a calm and comfortable place.

Daily Practice: Follow these steps each day:
- *Identify Core Values*: Reflect on what is most important to you. Write down 3-5 core values (e.g., honesty, kindness, growth).
- *Set Value-Aligned Goals*: For each core value, set a specific, achievable goal. Ensure these goals are SMART (Specific, Measurable, Achievable, Relevant, Time-bound).
- *Create an Action Plan*: Outline steps to achieve each goal. Identify necessary resources or support.
- *Daily Commitment*: Commit to taking at least one action each day that moves you closer to your value-aligned goals.

Daily Reflection: At the end of the day, reflect on your progress. Note any actions taken and their impact.

Weekly Review: At the end of each week, review your journal entries. Reflect on patterns and progress.

Consistency: Make this exercise a non-negotiable part of your daily routine.

Finding Purpose and Meaning

Purpose and meaning in life are not merely concepts to be understood but lived experiences that give depth to our existence. They are the bedrock upon which we can build a life of fulfillment, happiness, and resilience. **Clarifying your life's purpose** is akin to setting a compass for your journey through life, guiding your decisions, actions, and the paths you choose to explore. It is about discovering what truly matters to you, what ignites your passion, and what drives you to make a difference in the world around you.

Purpose-driven actions are those that align with this deeper understanding of your life's mission. They are the steps you take, big or small, that resonate with your core values and move you closer to achieving your goals. These actions imbue your daily life with significance, transforming routine tasks into meaningful contributions towards your larger vision. Whether it's choosing a career that reflects your passions, engaging in hobbies that bring you joy, or volunteering for causes close to your heart, every action becomes a building block in the edifice of your purposeful life.

To cultivate a life filled with purpose and meaning, begin by reflecting on moments that have brought you genuine joy and satisfaction. Consider the activities that make you lose track of time, the topics that spark your curiosity, and the dreams that fill you with excitement. These are clues to your unique purpose, signposts pointing towards paths worth exploring.

Next, set aside time for regular self-reflection. This can take the form of journaling, meditation, or quiet contemplation. Use these moments to connect with your inner self, to listen to your heart's desires, and to clarify your vision for your life. Ask yourself what legacy you wish to leave behind, how you want to be remembered, and what impact you want to have on the world.

Engage in purpose-driven actions by setting specific, actionable goals aligned with your purpose. Break these goals down into small, manageable steps, and celebrate your progress along the way. Remember, the pursuit of purpose is not a race but a lifelong journey, one that is continually evolving as you grow and learn.

Finally, surround yourself with people who support and share your vision. Building a community of like-minded individuals can provide encouragement, inspiration, and accountability as you pursue your purpose. These connections not only enrich your own life but also amplify your impact, creating ripples of positive change that extend far beyond yourself.

In embracing your purpose and infusing your actions with meaning, you unlock the door to a life of deeper fulfillment and joy. This journey towards purpose is not always easy, but it is undoubtedly rewarding, offering a wellspring of motivation, resilience, and satisfaction that can sustain you through life's challenges. By committing to live in alignment with your purpose, you forge a path that is uniquely yours, a path that leads to a richer, more vibrant life.

Clarifying Your Life's Purpose

Reflecting on the essence of **clarifying your life's purpose** involves delving deep into the core of your being to uncover the passions and motivations that drive you. It's about peeling back the layers of societal expectations, familial pressures, and personal doubts to reveal the true aspirations of your heart. This process requires courage, honesty, and a willingness to confront the aspects of your life that may not align with your innermost desires. The clarity that comes from understanding your purpose can illuminate your path, providing direction and a sense of fulfillment as you navigate the complexities of daily life. It transforms every decision, action, and thought, aligning them with a greater vision that transcends the mundane and touches the extraordinary.

To achieve this level of understanding, **engage in deep introspection**. Start by asking yourself probing questions that go beyond the surface. What activities make you feel most alive? When do you find yourself completely absorbed in the moment, losing all track of time? These moments of flow are indicators of your passions, hinting at areas where your purpose may lie. Consider the issues that stir your heart, the injustices that provoke a strong reaction, and the causes you are drawn to support. These emotional responses are signposts, guiding you toward your purpose.

Creating a vision board can be a powerful tool in this journey. It allows you to visualize your aspirations, goals, and dreams in a tangible form. By selecting images, quotes, and symbols that resonate with your vision for your life, you create a physical representation of your purpose. This board serves as a constant reminder of your direction, helping you to remain focused and inspired as you work towards your goals.

Journaling is another invaluable practice for clarifying your purpose. It provides a safe space to explore your thoughts, feelings, and desires without judgment.

Through regular writing, patterns begin to emerge, revealing your deepest values and the themes that consistently appear in your life. These insights can be crucial in understanding what drives you and how you can align your life with your purpose.

Seeking feedback from those you trust can offer new perspectives on your strengths, talents, and potential areas of impact. Sometimes, others can see aspects of ourselves that we are blind to. Engaging in conversations about your aspirations, fears, and dreams with trusted friends or mentors can open your eyes to possibilities you hadn't considered and help refine your understanding of your purpose.

Remember, **clarifying your life's purpose** is not a one-time event but a continuous process of growth and discovery. Your purpose may evolve as you gain new experiences, insights, and wisdom. It's important to remain open to this evolution, allowing your purpose to unfold and adapt over time. By committing to this ongoing journey of self-discovery, you ensure that your life remains aligned with your deepest values and aspirations, leading to a more fulfilling and meaningful existence.

In embracing these practices with an open heart and mind, you gradually build a life that not only reflects your true self but also empowers you to make a significant impact on the world around you. This alignment between inner purpose and external actions brings a profound sense of satisfaction and joy, marking the path toward a deeply rewarding life.

Purpose-Driven Actions for Fulfillment

Engaging in **purpose-driven actions** for fulfillment requires a blend of self-awareness, strategic planning, and an unwavering commitment to personal growth. The foundation of this approach lies in the deep understanding of one's core values and the relentless pursuit of goals that resonate with these values. It's about making conscious choices every day that align with what is most meaningful to you, thereby infusing your life with a sense of purpose and direction. This alignment is crucial for not just achieving fulfillment but also for nurturing resilience and joy in the journey of life.

To actualize this alignment, start by **breaking down your goals** into actionable steps that are both realistic and challenging. This process transforms lofty aspirations into tangible tasks, making the journey towards fulfillment feel more manageable and less overwhelming. It's important to approach this with a mindset that is open to learning and adaptation, recognizing that goals and paths may shift as you evolve. Embrace these changes as part of the growth process, keeping your core values as your guiding star.

Cultivating a supportive community plays a pivotal role in sustaining purpose-driven actions. Surround yourself with individuals who not only share similar values but also encourage and challenge you to pursue your goals. This network can provide invaluable feedback, motivation, and accountability, three elements that are essential for long-term fulfillment. Remember, the strength of your relationships often reflects the strength of your commitment to your purpose.

Incorporating **regular self-reflection** into your routine is another key strategy. This practice allows you to pause, assess your progress, and recalibrate your actions as needed. Use this time to celebrate your wins, no matter how small, and to learn from the setbacks. Self-reflection fosters a growth mindset, empowering you to view challenges as opportunities to learn and to strengthen your resolve.

Practicing gratitude is also integral to purpose-driven actions for fulfillment. By acknowledging and appreciating what you have achieved and the progress you've made, you cultivate a positive outlook that fuels further action. Gratitude shifts your focus from what's lacking to what's abundant, thereby enhancing your resilience and motivation.

Lastly, **embrace the power of giving back**. Purpose-driven actions often lead to the realization that true fulfillment comes not just from achieving personal goals but from contributing to something greater than oneself. Whether it's through mentorship, volunteering, or other forms of service, giving back adds a layer of meaning to your actions that is both enriching and humbling.

By integrating these strategies into your life, you build a framework for living that is rich in purpose, fulfillment, and joy. Each step taken with intention and alignment with your core values contributes to a life that is not only successful by your own standards but also meaningful and impactful. Remember, fulfillment is not a destination but a way of living, a continuous journey that unfolds with each purpose-driven action you take.

Exercise n.8: Purpose Statement Creation Exercise

Objective: Write a personal purpose statement to guide actions.
Type: Reflection and Writing Exercise
Duration: One-time session, for at least 30-45 minutes.

Instructions:

Set Aside Time: Dedicate 30-45 minutes for this exercise. Choose a time when you can reflect deeply without interruptions.

Find a Quiet Space: Choose a calm and comfortable place where you won't be disturbed.

Reflection Prompts: Answer the following prompts to gain clarity on your purpose:

- *Identify Core Values*: Reflect on what is most important to you. Write down 3-5 core values (e.g., honesty, integrity, kindness, growth).

- *Reflect on Passions*: Consider activities, topics, or causes you are passionate about. Write these down.

- *Consider Strengths*: Identify your strengths and talents. Write down what you are naturally good at.

- *Define Impact*: Think about the impact you want to have on those around you. Write down how you want to contribute to your community.

Writing Your Purpose Statement: Using your reflections, craft a concise purpose statement that encapsulates your core values, passions, strengths, and desired impact. Aim for 1-2 sentences that are clear and inspiring.

Review and Refine: Read your purpose statement aloud and refine it until it resonates deeply with you. Ensure it feels authentic and motivating.

Daily Reflection: Each day, take a moment to read your purpose statement. Reflect on how your actions and decisions align with it.

Periodic Review: Revisit and review your purpose statement periodically (e.g., monthly, or quarterly) to ensure it continues to reflect your evolving values and goals.

Developing Resilient Habits

D eveloping resilient habits is akin to laying a strong foundation for a house that is meant to withstand storms and earthquakes. It begins with the understanding that resilience is not an inherent trait but a skill that can be honed through consistent practice and dedication. The journey towards cultivating these habits requires an initial commitment to self-improvement and the willingness to step out of one's comfort zone. This process involves identifying behaviors that contribute to a resilient mindset and integrating them into daily life.

The first step in this endeavor is to establish a clear and realistic goal-setting strategy. Goals should be specific, measurable, achievable, relevant, and time-bound (SMART). This approach ensures that objectives are not only clear but also attainable, which is crucial for maintaining motivation and focus. For instance, instead of setting a vague goal like "I want to be more resilient," a SMART goal would be "I will practice mindfulness for 10 minutes every day for the next month to improve my stress response." This specificity provides a clear roadmap and makes it easier to track progress.

Another vital aspect of developing resilient habits is the cultivation of a positive mindset. This doesn't mean ignoring the negative aspects of life or pretending that problems don't exist. Rather, it's about adopting a more optimistic outlook that focuses on solutions rather than problems. It involves recognizing that setbacks are temporary and that you have the strength and resources to overcome them. One effective way to foster a positive mindset is through the practice of gratitude. By regularly reflecting on and appreciating what you have, you can shift your perspective from one of scarcity to one of abundance, which is a powerful catalyst for resilience.

Building a strong support network is also essential for resilience. Surrounding yourself with people who believe in you, encourage you, and offer constructive feedback can significantly enhance your ability to bounce back from challenges. These relationships provide emotional support, practical advice, and a sense of belonging, all of which are invaluable during tough times. It's important to actively nurture these connections by being a supportive presence in the lives of others as well, creating a mutual support system.

In addition to these strategies, integrating mindfulness and self-care into your routine can greatly contribute to resilience. Mindfulness practices, such as meditation, deep breathing, and yoga, help in cultivating a state of calm and presence, allowing you to face challenges with clarity and composure. Similarly, self-care activities that promote physical, emotional, and mental well-being, such as exercise, healthy eating, and adequate sleep, equip your body and mind to handle stress more effectively.

As you embark on this journey, remember that developing resilient habits is a gradual process that requires patience, perseverance, and self-compassion. It's normal to encounter setbacks and to sometimes revert to old patterns of behavior. What matters most is your commitment to getting back on track and learning from these experiences. Each step forward, no matter how small, is a victory in building a more resilient self.

Embracing failure as a stepping stone to resilience is another critical aspect of this journey. Instead of viewing setbacks as insurmountable obstacles, reframe them as opportunities for learning and growth. This shift in perspective encourages a growth mindset, where challenges are seen not as threats but as chances to expand your abilities and knowledge. For example, if a project at work does not go as planned, instead of dwelling on the failure, analyze what went wrong and what can be learned from the experience. This approach not only builds resilience but also fosters innovation and creativity.

Practicing flexibility and adaptability is equally important. In a world that is constantly changing, the ability to adjust your thoughts, behaviors, and actions in response to new situations is invaluable. This means being open to new ideas, willing to change course when necessary, and able to cope with uncertainty. Developing this kind of agility can start with small steps, such as trying out a new hobby or changing your routine. Over time, these small acts of flexibility can build your confidence in handling larger life changes.

Commitment to ongoing self-improvement is the bedrock of resilient habits. This entails seeking out new knowledge, skills, and experiences that contribute to your growth. It also means being proactive in identifying areas of weakness and taking steps to strengthen them. Whether it's through reading, taking courses, or seeking mentorship, continuous learning is a powerful tool for resilience. It keeps you engaged and motivated, and it ensures that you are always prepared to face whatever challenges come your way.

Remember, resilience is not just about surviving tough times but thriving despite them. It's about harnessing the power of your experiences to create a stronger, more adaptable, and more fulfilled self. This journey is deeply personal and unique to each individual, so be patient with yourself and honor your progress, no matter how incremental it may seem.

To further support your development of resilient habits, consider integrating regular feedback mechanisms into your life. This could involve setting aside time for weekly self-reflection, soliciting feedback from trusted friends or colleagues, or keeping a resilience journal where you document challenges, successes, and the lessons learned along the way. These practices not only reinforce your growth but also provide valuable insights into your personal resilience journey.

Lastly, celebrate your successes. Recognizing and rewarding yourself for the resilience you demonstrate in facing life's challenges is crucial. Celebrations can be as simple as taking a moment to acknowledge your hard work, treating yourself to something you enjoy, or sharing your achievements with loved ones. These moments of celebration reinforce the positive behaviors that contribute to resilience, making them more likely to become ingrained habits.

By incorporating these strategies into your daily life, you lay the foundation for a resilient mindset that can withstand life's challenges. Resilience is a dynamic process, one that evolves as you gain new insights, experiences, and strengths. With each step forward, you not only build resilience but also pave the way for a life characterized by growth, fulfillment, and inner strength.

The Power of Habit Reprogramming

Habit reprogramming is a critical step in the journey towards developing resilient habits, focusing on the concept that our daily routines are composed of habits that can either propel us towards our goals or hold us back. The essence of habit reprogramming lies in identifying the habits that don't serve us well and systematically replacing them with ones that do. This process begins with a keen awareness of our current habits, particularly those we perform subconsciously. By bringing these habits into the realm of conscious thought, we can evaluate their impact on our lives.

The first actionable step in habit reprogramming is to **maintain a habit journal**. This involves documenting your daily routines, noting down each habit and the feelings or outcomes associated with it. This practice shines a light on patterns that may have been invisible, enabling a targeted approach to change. For instance, if you discover a habit of scrolling through social media first thing in the morning leads to feelings of inadequacy or time wasted, this awareness is the first step towards change.

Next, **identify the triggers** that lead to the undesirable habit. Triggers can be emotional, such as feeling stressed or bored, or situational, like sitting on the couch after work. Understanding these triggers is crucial because it allows you to anticipate and intercept the habit loop before it starts. Replacing a negative habit with a positive one requires you to insert a new routine in response to the old trigger. If stress triggers mindless snacking, try a brief meditation or a quick walk instead.

Creating an environment that supports your new habits is equally important. Environment plays a significant role in habit formation. If your goal is to read more instead of watching TV in the evenings, you might place a book on your nightstand or in your living room where you usually sit to watch TV. Making the desired habit easier to do and the undesired habit harder is a powerful strategy in habit reprogramming.

Building a support system around your new habits can significantly enhance your success rate. Share your goals with friends or family members who can hold you accountable, or better yet, find someone with a similar goal and work on it together. This not only provides motivation but also creates a sense of responsibility towards someone else, which can be a powerful motivator.

Rewarding yourself for small victories plays a critical role in reinforcing the new habit. The brain is wired to repeat actions that make it feel good, so creating positive associations with your new habits is crucial. If you're trying to establish a habit of morning exercise, treat yourself to a nice breakfast or a relaxing shower afterward. These rewards help solidify the new habit loop.

Lastly, **be patient and kind to yourself**. Habit reprogramming is not an overnight process. It requires time, persistence, and sometimes, dealing with setbacks. When you slip into old habits, view it as a learning opportunity rather than a failure. Analyze what led to the slip and how you can adjust your strategy moving forward. Remember, resilience is not about never failing; it's about bouncing back and not giving up.

By applying these strategies, you can reprogram your habits, making them allies in your quest for a more resilient and fulfilling life. Each small change in your daily routine can have a profound impact over time, leading to significant personal growth and transformation.

Understanding Triggers and Cues

Recognizing triggers and cues is a crucial aspect of habit reprogramming, as these are the signals that initiate a habit loop. A trigger can be an emotional state, time of day, visual cue, or any event that leads to the automatic execution of a routine. For example, feeling stressed (trigger) might lead to biting nails (habit). The key to altering habits lies in identifying these triggers and either avoiding them, altering them, or replacing the negative habit with a more positive one in response to the trigger.

Cues, on the other hand, are slightly different but related concepts. They are the specific signals that prompt a certain behavior. For instance, seeing a pack of cigarettes on a table (cue) might trigger a smoking habit. Understanding both triggers and cues is essential for anyone looking to change their behavior patterns.

To begin with, one practical step is to keep a detailed log of your habits for at least a week. Note down the habit you want to change, what happened right before you engaged in that habit (the trigger), and any cues that might have contributed to it. This could include your emotional state, the time, people you were with, or any environmental factors. Over time, patterns will emerge, revealing the triggers and cues that are most influential in your life.

Once you've identified your triggers and cues, the next step is to create a plan for dealing with them. If possible, remove the cue from your environment. For example, if you're trying to eat healthier but find yourself snacking on junk food you see in the kitchen, remove the junk food from your sight. If avoiding the trigger isn't possible, as in the case of stress, plan a different response to it. Instead of reaching for a cigarette or junk food when stressed, you could plan to take a short walk, practice deep breathing, or engage in a quick meditation session.

It's also beneficial to replace a negative habit with a positive one that fulfills the same need. If you find that boredom is a trigger for mindless scrolling on social media, you might decide to read a book or engage in a hobby like drawing or playing an instrument whenever you feel bored. This way, you're not just trying to stop a habit but are instead replacing it with something that is both positive and fulfills a similar need.

Building new habits also requires patience and persistence. It's common to slip up in the early stages. When this happens, it's important not to be too hard on yourself. Instead, view it as valuable information about the strength of your triggers and cues and an opportunity to refine your strategy. Remember, every attempt at changing a habit, whether successful or not, is a step forward in your understanding of yourself and your habit loops.

Creating an environment that supports your new habits is crucial. This might mean rearranging your space to make positive habits easier to perform or surrounding yourself with people who support your goals. Additionally, leveraging technology can be a powerful ally. There are numerous apps designed to help track habits, remind you to engage in positive behaviors, and provide a platform for logging triggers and cues.

Ultimately, the process of understanding triggers and cues is about gaining deeper insight into how your habits are formed and maintained. With this understanding, you can begin to take deliberate steps toward changing your behavior in a way that aligns with your values and goals. This approach not only leads to the development of resilient habits but also empowers you to take control of your actions and, by extension, your life.

Replacing Negative Habits

Replacing negative habits with positive ones begins with a conscious decision to improve one's life. This transformative process requires patience, dedication, and a strategic approach. The first step is to identify the negative habits that are holding you back. This involves a deep and honest self-assessment, where you take stock of your daily routines and behaviors to pinpoint those that are detrimental to your well-being. Once identified, the next step is to understand the triggers that lead to these habits. Triggers can be emotional, such as stress or boredom, or situational, like a specific time of day or being in a particular place.

Understanding these triggers is crucial because it allows you to develop strategies to avoid them or to respond differently when they occur. For instance, if stress triggers a negative habit, introducing stress-reduction techniques such as deep breathing exercises or meditation can be beneficial. Similarly, if boredom leads to mindless scrolling on social media, planning engaging activities or hobbies to fill your time can serve as an effective countermeasure.

Replacing a negative habit with a positive one also involves setting clear, achievable goals. Instead of vague resolutions like "I will stop procrastinating," opt for specific goals such as "I will dedicate 30 minutes each morning to work on my most important task." This specificity makes the goal more tangible and easier to stick to. Additionally, breaking down larger goals into smaller, manageable tasks can help maintain motivation and provide a sense of accomplishment as each task is completed.

Accountability plays a significant role in habit change. Sharing your goals with a friend, family member, or a support group can increase your chances of success. These accountability partners can provide encouragement, celebrate your wins, and offer support during challenging times. Furthermore, tracking your progress can be incredibly motivating. Whether it's marking a calendar for each day you successfully avoid a negative habit or keeping a journal to reflect on your journey, seeing evidence of your progress reinforces your commitment to change.

Celebrating wins, no matter how small, is essential. Rewarding yourself for making progress reinforces the positive behavior and makes the journey more enjoyable. These rewards can be as simple as taking a moment to acknowledge your effort, enjoying a favorite treat, or doing something you love.

Lastly, it's important to be patient and kind to yourself throughout this process. Changing ingrained habits takes time, and setbacks are a normal part of the journey. Instead of viewing setbacks as failures, see them as opportunities to learn and grow. Each attempt provides valuable insights into what works and what doesn't, allowing you to refine your approach and continue moving forward.

By understanding the triggers of negative habits, setting specific goals, seeking accountability, tracking progress, celebrating wins, and practicing self-compassion, you can replace negative habits with positive ones. This not only leads to personal growth and improved well-being but also empowers you to live a more intentional and fulfilling life.

Exercise n.9: Habit Swap Exercise

Objective: Identify a negative habit and replace it with a positive one.
Type: Habit-Building Exercise
Duration: Daily, for at least 10-15 minutes.

Instructions:
Set Aside Time: Dedicate 10-15 minutes each day.

Find a Quiet Space: Choose a calm and comfortable place.

Daily Practice: Follow these steps each day:
* *Identify a Negative Habit*: Reflect on a habit you want to change. Write down the habit and why it is negative.
* *Understand the Trigger*: Identify the trigger or situation that leads to this negative habit.
* *Choose a Positive Replacement*: Select a positive habit to replace the negative one. Write down the new habit and why you chose it.
* *Create an Action Plan*: Outline steps to implement the positive habit. Identify any resources or support you might need.
* *Commit to the Swap*: Make a commitment to replace the negative habit with the positive one each time the trigger occurs.

Daily Reflection: At the end of the day, reflect on your progress. Note any instances where you successfully replaced the negative habit and any challenges faced.

Weekly Review: At the end of each week, review your journal entries. Reflect on patterns and progress.

Consistency: Make this habit swap exercise a non-negotiable part of your daily routine.

Building Lasting Positive Habits

To ensure the formation of lasting positive habits, it's crucial to integrate these new practices into the very fabric of your daily life. This means creating an environment that supports your goals and reduces the likelihood of reverting to old patterns. For instance, if your aim is to cultivate a habit of reading before bed instead of scrolling through social media, consider keeping a book on your nightstand as a visual cue and charging your phone in another room to minimize temptation.

Engagement with the process is another cornerstone of building lasting habits. This involves celebrating the small victories along the way. Did you choose to walk instead of taking the car for a short distance? Acknowledge this choice and allow yourself to feel proud. These moments of recognition fuel your motivation and reinforce the positive behavior.

Consistency is key, yet flexibility should not be overlooked. Life is unpredictable, and rigidly adhering to a habit without room for adjustment can lead to frustration and eventual abandonment of the goal. If you miss a day of exercise due to unforeseen circumstances, rather than viewing it as a failure, adapt your schedule to include a walk during lunch the next day. This approach maintains the momentum of habit formation without the pressure of perfection.

Social support plays a pivotal role in habit sustainability. Surround yourself with people who share or support your goals. Whether it's a running club, a book group, or a friend with whom you can share your progress, these relationships provide encouragement and accountability. Sharing your goals with others not only commits you to these objectives but also opens the door for support that can keep you on track.

Reflection and adjustment are necessary components of any habit formation process. Regularly assess how your new habits are impacting your life. Are you feeling more energized since you started exercising in the morning? Has preparing your meals in advance reduced the stress of deciding what to eat every day? This reflection can affirm the value of your new habits or indicate when adjustments are needed to better align with your goals.

Incorporating technology can also aid in building lasting habits. Numerous apps are designed to track progress, remind you of your goals, and even connect you with a community of like-minded individuals. Utilizing these tools can provide a modern approach to traditional habit formation techniques, offering both convenience and a source of motivation.

By creating supportive environments, engaging with the process, maintaining consistency while allowing for flexibility, seeking social support, reflecting and adjusting, and incorporating technology, you can build and sustain positive habits that contribute to a more intentional and fulfilling life. These strategies, when applied thoughtfully and consistently, pave the way for lasting change and personal growth.

21-Day Habit Building Challenge

Embarking on the 21-Day Habit Building Challenge is a powerful way to solidify the principles of lasting positive habits into your daily routine. This challenge is designed to help you apply the strategies discussed earlier, focusing on consistency, reflection, and adaptation to foster habits that contribute to a more intentional and fulfilling life. Over the next three weeks, you'll engage in a structured yet flexible program that encourages you to take actionable steps towards habit formation, leveraging the power of small, daily actions to create significant, long-term change.

The first week is all about setting the foundation. Select one positive habit you wish to develop that aligns with your core values and purpose. This could be as simple as dedicating 15 minutes each morning to meditation or as challenging as replacing an hour of evening television with reading. The key is to choose a habit that resonates with your personal growth goals and is realistically achievable within your current lifestyle. During this week, focus on the cues that trigger your habit and the rewards you'll receive from sticking to it. Document your observations, feelings, and any resistance you encounter in a journal. This reflection is crucial for understanding your habit on a deeper level and preparing for the challenges ahead.

In the second week, your goal is to deepen the integration of your new habit into your daily life. This involves identifying and overcoming obstacles that may have surfaced during the first week. Perhaps you found that morning meditation was consistently interrupted by early work emails. In response, you might decide to wake up 30 minutes earlier or to meditate during your lunch break instead. Adaptation is a critical skill in habit formation, allowing you to maintain progress even when faced with unexpected challenges. This week, also begin to explore the role of accountability by sharing your goal with a friend or joining an online community of individuals with similar objectives. The support and encouragement from others can be incredibly motivating, providing an extra layer of commitment to your habit.

The final week of the challenge is about reflection and celebration. By now, your new habit should be taking root, but it's important to recognize that habit formation is an ongoing process. Reflect on the progress you've made and how the habit has impacted your life. Are you feeling more energized or focused? Have you noticed improvements in your mood or stress levels? Acknowledging these changes, no matter how small, reinforces the value of your efforts. Celebrate your successes and consider setting a new goal for the next 21 days to continue building on your momentum.

Throughout the challenge, remember to practice self-compassion. There will be days when you falter, and that's okay. What matters most is your ability to learn from these experiences and to persevere. Each day offers a new opportunity to strengthen your resolve and to inch closer to the person you aspire to be. By approaching this challenge with an open mind and a committed heart, you're not just developing a new habit; you're forging a path towards a more empowered and authentic life.

Exercise n.10: 21-Day Habit Tracker Exercise

Objective: Reinforce a new habit and get consistency over 21 days.
Type: Tracking Exercise
Duration: Daily, for 21 days, see examples below.

Instructions:
Set Aside Time: Dedicate a few minutes each day to track your progress. Consistency is key, so try to do it at the same time each day.

Choose a New Habit: Identify a new habit you want to develop. Ensure it is specific, achievable, and beneficial. Write down the habit and why you chose it.

Create a Habit Tracker: Use a notebook, a digital document, or a habit-tracking app to create your 21-day tracker. Include the following columns:
- Date
- Habit done (Yes/No)
- Notes/Reflections

Daily Tracking: Each day, mark whether you completed the habit. Use the notes section to reflect on your experience, any challenges faced, and how you felt.

Weekly Review: At the end of each week, review your tracker. Reflect on your progress, any patterns you notice, and write a summary of your observations and any adjustments needed.

Consistency: Make tracking your new habit a non-negotiable part of your daily routine to foster consistency and reinforce the new behavior.

Example Entry:
Chosen Habit: Drink 8 glasses of water daily.
Reason: To improve hydration and overall health.

Example Habit Tracker:

Date	Habit done	Notes / Reflections
Oct 1, 2023	Yes	Felt more energized and less hungry
Oct 2, 2023	Yes	Struggled in the afternoon, set reminders
Oct 3, 2023	No	Busy day, forgot to track water intake
....		

Tracking Progress, Celebrating Wins

Tracking progress and celebrating wins are critical components in the development of resilient habits, serving as both a motivational tool and a method for self-assessment. To effectively track progress, it's advisable to employ a method that resonates with your personal style and preferences. For some, this may involve a digital app that logs daily activities, habits, and milestones. These apps often provide visual representations of progress, such as charts and graphs, making it easy to see at a glance how far you have come. For others, a more tactile approach, such as a physical journal or planner, can be more satisfying. Writing down accomplishments by hand can create a stronger psychological imprint of your achievements, enhancing the sense of satisfaction and progress.

Incorporate regular check-ins with yourself to review your progress. This could be a weekly or monthly sit-down where you go through your tracking method of choice to evaluate how well you are sticking to your habits. During these sessions, ask yourself questions like, "What challenges did I face in maintaining my habit?" and "What strategies worked best for me in overcoming these challenges?" These reflective questions encourage a deeper understanding of your habit formation process and help identify areas for improvement.

Celebrating wins, no matter their size, plays a crucial role in reinforcing the positive changes you are making. When you reach a milestone, no matter how small, take the time to celebrate. This could mean treating yourself to a favorite activity, purchasing something small that you've been wanting, or simply taking a moment to acknowledge your effort and success. These celebrations act as positive reinforcement, making you more likely to stick with your habits in the long run.

It's also beneficial to share your successes with others. Whether it's a close friend, family member, or an online community, sharing your progress can provide an additional layer of accountability and support. The encouragement and validation received from others can be incredibly motivating, pushing you to continue striving towards your goals.

Remember, the path to building resilient habits is not linear. There will be setbacks and days when your motivation wanes. During these times, it's important to rely on your tracking and the habit of celebrating wins to remind yourself of how far you've come. Reflect on the progress you've made rather than focusing solely on the setbacks. This shift in perspective can reignite your motivation and help you maintain a positive outlook.

Furthermore, adaptability is key in tracking progress and celebrating wins. If you find that a certain method of tracking isn't working for you or that your way of celebrating doesn't bring you joy, be open to trying something new. The goal is to find what best supports your journey to building and sustaining positive habits.

In essence, the practices of tracking progress and celebrating wins are not just about acknowledging what you've accomplished. They are about creating and maintaining a mindset that values growth, recognizes effort, and understands the importance of small steps in achieving lasting change. By integrating these practices into your routine, you reinforce your commitment to developing resilient habits that contribute to a more intentional and fulfilling life.

Exercise n.11: Weekly Reflection on Progress Exercise

Objective: Assess progress, celebrate wins, and adjust goals.
Type: Reflection and Tracking
Duration: Weekly, for at least 15-20 minutes.

Instructions:

Set Aside Time: Dedicate 15-20 minutes at the end of each week for this exercise. Consistency is key, so try to do it at the same time each week (e.g., Sunday evening).

Find a Quiet Space: Choose a calm and comfortable place where you won't be disturbed.

Weekly Reflection Prompts: Answer the following prompts each week:
- *Review Goals*: List the goals you set for the week. Reflect on whether you achieved them. If not, consider what obstacles you encountered.
- *Celebrate Wins*: Identify and celebrate any achievements, no matter how small. Reflect on what went well and why.
- *Assess Challenges*: Reflect on any challenges or setbacks you faced. Consider what you learned from these experiences.
- *Adjust Goals*: Based on your reflections, adjust your goals for the upcoming week. Ensure they are realistic and aligned with your long-term objectives.
- *Plan Actions*: Outline specific actions you will take to achieve your adjusted goals. Identify any resources or support you might need.

Document Your Reflections: Use a notebook, a digital document, or a journaling app to record your weekly reflections. This will help you track your progress over time.

Consistency: Make this weekly reflection exercise a non-negotiable part of your routine to foster continuous improvement and personal growth.

Intentionality in Everyday Actions

Living each day with **intentionality** transforms the mundane into the meaningful, turning everyday actions into powerful steps towards personal fulfillment. By choosing to live intentionally, you affirm your values and purpose with every decision you make, from the moment you wake up to the moment you rest your head at night. This deliberate approach to life requires mindfulness and a commitment to aligning your actions with your core values, ensuring that each choice reflects what truly matters to you.

To cultivate **intentionality in everyday actions**, start by setting clear intentions for your day. Before the busyness sweeps you away, take a few moments each morning to reflect on what you wish to achieve and how you want to feel by the end of the day. This could be as simple as deciding to approach your tasks with a positive attitude or as specific as completing a project that aligns with your long-term goals.

Prioritize your tasks based on their significance to your values and purpose. It's easy to get caught up in the urgency of daily demands, but by focusing on what's truly important, you ensure that your energy is invested in activities that bring you closer to your goals. This might mean saying no to requests that don't align with your intentions or delegating tasks that distract from your priorities.

Mindfulness plays a crucial role in living intentionally. Throughout the day, regularly pause to bring your attention back to the present moment. This practice helps you stay focused on your current task and reduces the likelihood of mindless behavior. Whether you're eating, working, or spending time with loved ones, be fully present, savoring the experience and ensuring that it aligns with your intended path.

Reflection at the end of the day is equally important. Consider what actions were in harmony with your values and which ones were not. This isn't about self-judgment but about learning and adjusting your approach to be more intentional tomorrow. Celebrate your successes, no matter how small, and forgive yourself for any missteps, viewing them as opportunities for growth.

Habit formation is a powerful tool for embedding intentionality into your life. By establishing routines that reflect your values and goals, you make it easier to live intentionally without constant conscious effort. For instance, if health is a core value, a habit of morning exercise or preparing nutritious meals becomes a daily reaffirmation of that value. Likewise, if lifelong learning is important to you, dedicating time each day to read or explore new ideas can be a fulfilling habit.

Incorporating **gratitude** into your daily routine enhances the impact of living intentionally. Acknowledging the good in your life, the progress you're making, and the people who support you, shifts your focus from what's lacking to what's abundant. This positive mindset fuels motivation and contentment, making it easier to pursue your intentions with joy and resilience.

Accountability can significantly boost your efforts to live intentionally. Share your intentions with someone you trust or find a community of like-minded individuals. This support network can offer encouragement, share insights, and help you stay on track when distractions arise.

Finally, embrace **adaptability**. While living intentionally requires planning and reflection, be open to the unexpected. Life is unpredictable, and sometimes the most meaningful experiences come from spontaneous decisions. By staying true to your values while remaining flexible, you can navigate life's surprises without losing sight of your intentions.

By integrating these strategies into your daily life, you empower yourself to lead a life of purpose, fulfillment, and intentional action. Each day becomes an opportunity to manifest your values, pursue your goals, and deepen your connections, contributing to a richer, more meaningful existence.

Exercise n.12: Accountability Check-In Exercise

Objective: Stay motivated with weekly check-ins with a friend or mentor.
Type: Accountability Exercise
Duration: Weekly, for at least 15-20 minutes.

Instructions:
Choose an Accountability Partner: Select a supportive and reliable friend, mentor, or colleague willing to participate in weekly check-ins.

Set a Regular Meeting Time: Schedule a consistent time each week that works for both of you.

Prepare for the Check-In: Reflect on your week, considering goals, achievements, challenges, and adjustments needed.

Weekly Check-In Agenda:
- *Share Goals*: Discuss goals set for the week, achievements, and obstacles.
- *Celebrate Wins*: Celebrate any achievements, no matter how small.
- *Discuss Challenges*: Share challenges faced and lessons learned.
- *Set New Goals*: Set realistic goals for the upcoming week.
- *Plan Actions*: Outline specific actions to achieve new goals.
- *Provide Support*: Offer support and encouragement to your partner.

Document Your Progress: Use a notebook, digital document, or journaling app to record your weekly check-ins.

Consistency: Make this check-in a non-negotiable part of your routine to stay motivated and on track.

Practicing **consistency** and **commitment** is paramount in transforming your life through the development of resilient habits. These two principles act as the backbone for any meaningful change, providing the structure and perseverance needed to overcome the inevitable challenges that will arise. To embody these values, it's important to establish a clear, actionable plan that aligns with your personal goals and values. As James Clear highlights in *Atomic Habits*, starting small is key. Setting 'atomic' goals, like reading just one page or meditating for one minute, is enough to build momentum and make consistency manageable. This begins with setting specific, measurable objectives that offer a roadmap to guide your actions. For instance, if your goal is to cultivate a practice of mindfulness, you might commit to meditating for ten minutes every morning. This precise goal not only makes the habit tangible but also provides a daily reminder of your commitment to personal growth.

Real-life examples demonstrate how powerful visual cues can be for consistency. Comedian Jerry Seinfeld, for example, used a *'Don't Break the Chain'* method, marking an 'X' on his calendar every day he wrote jokes. Over time, this growing chain of X's became a motivator to keep going. Using a calendar or habit-tracking app can have the same effect, making progress visible and encouraging you to stick with your goals.

Accountability enhances the power of consistency and commitment. Sharing your goals with a trusted friend or family member can offer an external source of motivation, pushing you to adhere to your commitments even when your internal resolve wanes. Additionally, leveraging technology through habit-tracking apps can offer a modern approach to monitoring your progress. These platforms often feature reminders, motivational quotes, and the ability to track streaks of consistency, serving as a digital accountability partner in your journey toward self-improvement.

Creating a vision board is another way to reinforce your goals. Fill a board with images, quotes, and symbols representing what you want to achieve, and place it somewhere you'll see daily. A vision board serves as a powerful visual reminder of your intentions and helps keep your motivation strong by making your aspirations feel tangible.

Creating a **supportive environment** is another critical strategy. This involves removing temptations that may lead you astray and surrounding yourself with cues that reinforce your new habits. If your goal is to read more, for example, placing a book on your nightstand where it's easily visible can serve as a constant reminder of your commitment. Similarly, if reducing screen time before bed is a priority, charging your phone outside the bedroom eliminates the temptation to scroll through social media, making it easier to stick to your intended habit.

Flexibility within the framework of consistency and commitment allows you to adapt to life's unpredictability without abandoning your goals. Understanding that there will be days when external factors disrupt your routine is crucial. Instead of viewing these disruptions as failures, see them as opportunities to practice resilience and flexibility. If you miss a morning meditation, for example, rather than letting this derail your progress, find a brief moment later in the day to engage in mindfulness. This adaptable mindset ensures that you maintain the essence of your commitment without being rigidly tied to a specific schedule.

Celebrating progress, no matter how small, is essential in nurturing your motivation and reinforcing your commitment. Acknowledging achievements serves as a powerful reminder of your capability to enact change. Whether it's marking a week of consistent meditation or recognizing an improvement in your stress levels, each celebration is a step toward solidifying your new habits. These moments of recognition are not just rewards but also integral components of the habit formation process, embedding the new behavior into your identity.

Furthermore, embedding **reflection** into your routine ensures that your actions remain aligned with your core values and goals. Regularly taking time to contemplate your progress, the challenges you've faced, and the strategies that have been most effective not only reinforces your commitment but also deepens your understanding of yourself. This introspective practice can illuminate areas for improvement and inspire adjustments to your approach, ensuring that your journey of personal growth continues to evolve in a direction that resonates with your aspirations.

Incorporating these strategies into your daily life demands a proactive stance towards personal development. By prioritizing consistency and commitment, you lay the groundwork for lasting change, transforming aspirations into reality. Each day presents a new opportunity to reinforce these principles through intentional action, gradually weaving the fabric of your transformed life. Through persistent effort, adaptability, and a celebration of each step forward, you cultivate a resilience that propels you toward your goals, embodying the empowered, authentic life you aspire to lead.

Maintaining Motivation and Accountability

Maintaining motivation and accountability in the development of resilient habits requires a multifaceted approach that touches on self-awareness, goal setting, and the cultivation of a supportive community. The allure of instant gratification often undermines our long-term objectives, making it crucial to anchor our actions in deeply held values and a clear vision of the life we wish to create. This vision serves not only as a beacon during moments of doubt but also as a framework within which we can measure our progress and adjust our strategies accordingly.

Psychologist Dr. Kristin Neff emphasizes the role of self-compassion in maintaining resilience. She explains that treating setbacks as learning opportunities, rather than failures, fosters a mindset of growth and perseverance. By approaching challenges with kindness toward ourselves, we create a resilient mental state that keeps us moving forward.

One effective method for maintaining motivation is to set incremental milestones that lead to larger goals. These milestones act as checkpoints, offering opportunities to celebrate progress and evaluate the effectiveness of our strategies. By breaking down our objectives into manageable tasks, we avoid the overwhelm that can accompany the pursuit of significant life changes. This approach also allows for the adjustment of tactics in response to feedback, ensuring that our efforts remain aligned with our ultimate goals.

Accountability plays a critical role in habit formation, serving as a powerful external motivator that can sustain our commitment when internal motivation wanes. In *Think and Grow Rich*, Napoleon Hill popularized the concept of 'mastermind groups'—communities of individuals who share similar goals and meet regularly to support each other. Surrounding yourself with like-minded people, whether in-person or online, can provide the encouragement you need to stay committed.

Engaging with a community of like-minded individuals who share similar aspirations can provide the encouragement and support needed to navigate challenges. Whether this community is found in online platforms, group coaching sessions, or informal gatherings, the sense of belonging and mutual support it offers is invaluable.

A very helpful approach is to practice daily visualization. Each morning, take a few minutes to imagine yourself achieving your goals—visualize the actions, emotions, and outcomes. This technique, used by athletes and high performers, primes your mind to succeed by mentally rehearsing the positive steps you will take.

Another aspect of accountability involves self-monitoring, which can be facilitated by tools such as journals, habit-tracking apps, or even simple checklists. These tools enable us to reflect on our daily actions, identify patterns that may be hindering our progress, and reinforce behaviors that move us closer to our goals. Regular self-reflection not only fosters a deeper connection with our inner selves but also empowers us to take ownership of our journey toward self-improvement.

Furthermore, the practice of self-compassion is essential in maintaining motivation and accountability. Recognizing that setbacks are an inevitable part of the growth process allows us to approach challenges with kindness and understanding, rather than self-criticism. This mindset shift is crucial, as it encourages resilience by framing obstacles as opportunities for learning and development, rather than as failures.

Incorporating visual reminders of our goals and values into our environment can also serve as a constant source of inspiration. Whether through vision boards, motivational quotes, or symbolic objects, these visual cues remind us of our larger purpose and help maintain focus on our long-term aspirations.

Ultimately, maintaining motivation and accountability in building resilient habits is a dynamic process that calls for flexibility, persistence, and openness to change. It involves staying committed through challenges, adjusting your approach as needed, and finding ways to reignite your motivation when it wanes. Incorporating these principles into daily life lays the groundwork for meaningful, lasting change. This process goes beyond simply reaching goals; it's about cultivating a stronger, more grounded self—living each day with purpose, inner strength, and a deep sense of fulfillment. In doing so, we empower ourselves to lead lives that truly reflect our values and aspirations.

Cultivating Emotional Resilience

E motional resilience is the bedrock upon which we can build a life of fulfillment and strength in the face of adversity. It's about developing a core of inner calm and steadfastness, regardless of the storms raging outside. To cultivate this invaluable trait, one must first understand that emotional resilience is not an innate quality bestowed upon a fortunate few but a skill that can be nurtured and developed over time. The process begins with recognizing our emotional triggers, those events or circumstances that elicit strong negative emotions within us. By identifying these triggers, we empower ourselves to anticipate and prepare for emotional responses rather than being blindsided by them.

Building a resilient mindset involves reframing our perspective towards challenges and stressors. Instead of viewing them as insurmountable obstacles, we can see them as opportunities for growth and learning. This shift in perspective doesn't happen overnight but through consistent practice and self-reflection. One effective strategy is to maintain a journal where you can document your emotional reactions to different situations and analyze them for patterns. This practice can illuminate how certain scenarios or interactions lead to specific emotional responses, providing valuable insights into how you can better manage similar situations in the future.

Another cornerstone of emotional resilience is the practice of mindfulness and meditation. These techniques help in grounding ourselves in the present moment, creating a space between our emotions and our reactions. By cultivating mindfulness, we learn not to be overwhelmed by our emotions but to observe them with detachment and curiosity. This doesn't mean suppressing our feelings but acknowledging them without judgment and allowing them to pass without letting them dictate our actions.

Self-care is also crucial in building emotional resilience. Often, we neglect our physical and mental well-being, especially during stressful times, not realizing that our emotional health is intrinsically linked to our overall wellness. Engaging in regular physical activity, ensuring adequate sleep, eating a balanced diet, and pursuing hobbies and activities that bring joy are all essential components of a resilient lifestyle. These practices not only improve our physical health but also enhance our emotional resilience by reducing stress and increasing our sense of well-being.

Furthermore, emotional resilience is bolstered by the support we receive from and give to others. Cultivating strong, positive relationships with family, friends, and colleagues provides a support network that can offer comfort and advice during difficult times. Sharing our experiences and feelings with trusted individuals can help in processing emotions and gaining different perspectives on our challenges. Conversely, offering support to others can reinforce our sense of purpose and connection, further strengthening our emotional resilience.

In the pursuit of emotional resilience, it's important to remember that setbacks and failures are part of the journey. They are not reflections of our worth but opportunities for learning and growth. Adopting a growth mindset, where challenges are seen as chances to develop and improve, can significantly enhance our capacity for resilience. This mindset encourages perseverance, adaptability, and a willingness to learn from every experience, qualities that are essential for building and maintaining emotional resilience.

By integrating these practices into our daily lives, we can begin to cultivate a deeper sense of emotional resilience that not only helps us navigate through life's challenges but also enables us to thrive and find joy in the journey.

Embracing vulnerability is another key aspect of cultivating emotional resilience. It involves the courage to face our fears, uncertainties, and feelings of insecurity without resorting to denial or avoidance. When we allow ourselves to be vulnerable, we open the door to genuine self-discovery and the opportunity to develop a more compassionate relationship with ourselves and others. This process of embracing vulnerability can be challenging, as it requires letting go of the need for control and the fear of judgment. However, it is through this openness that we can truly connect with our inner strength and the essence of who we are.

The role of gratitude in building emotional resilience cannot be overstated. Regularly practicing gratitude shifts our focus from what we lack to what we have, fostering a sense of abundance and well-being. This can be as simple as keeping a gratitude journal, where daily entries highlight the people, experiences, and aspects of our lives for which we are thankful. Over time, this practice cultivates an attitude of gratitude that can significantly buffer against the stress and negativity that life may throw our way.

Learning to set and maintain healthy boundaries is also crucial for emotional resilience. Boundaries help protect our energy and well-being by defining what is and isn't acceptable in our interactions and relationships. They allow us to say no without guilt, to ask for what we need, and to prioritize our own well-being without feeling selfish. Establishing clear boundaries is a form of self-respect and is essential for maintaining emotional balance and preventing burnout.

Incorporating acts of kindness and service into our lives enhances emotional resilience by reinforcing our sense of purpose and connection to others. Altruistic behavior has been shown to boost mood and self-esteem, reduce stress, and promote a sense of belonging. Whether it's volunteering, helping a neighbor, or simply offering a listening ear, acts of kindness can create a ripple effect of positivity that strengthens our emotional resilience.

Finally, the journey of cultivating emotional resilience is ongoing and ever evolving. It requires patience, persistence, and a commitment to personal growth. Each day presents new challenges and opportunities for strengthening our emotional resilience. By adopting a proactive and mindful approach to our emotional well-being, we equip ourselves with the tools to not only withstand life's adversities but to emerge from them stronger, more compassionate, and more empowered individuals.

As we integrate these practices into our daily routine, we gradually build a resilient mindset that enables us to face life's uncertainties with confidence and grace. The cultivation of emotional resilience is a deeply personal and transformative process, one that enriches our lives and enhances our capacity for joy, connection, and fulfillment.

Emotional Resilience Explained

Emotional resilience is essentially our ability to bounce back from stress, adversity, failure, challenges, or even trauma. It's not about avoiding these experiences, which are an inevitable part of life, but rather how we deal with them, learn from them, and move forward. At the core of developing emotional resilience is the understanding that our reactions to these situations significantly impact our overall well-being and the quality of our lives. **Building emotional resilience** involves cultivating a set of skills and attitudes that allow us to withstand life's ups and downs with grace and come out stronger on the other side.

One key aspect of emotional resilience is **self-awareness**. This means having a clear understanding of your thoughts, beliefs, emotions, and actions, and recognizing how they influence your reactions to stressful situations. Developing self-awareness can be achieved through practices like **mindfulness meditation**, which trains you to observe your thoughts and feelings without judgment, and **self-reflection**, which involves taking time to think about your experiences, behaviors, and responses to determine what you can learn from them.

Adaptability is another crucial component of emotional resilience. Life is unpredictable, and circumstances can change rapidly and without warning. Being adaptable means having the flexibility to adjust your strategies, plans, and even your thinking in response to new situations. It requires an open mind and a willingness to let go of old patterns that no longer serve you.

Problem-solving skills are also essential for emotional resilience. When faced with a challenge, resilient individuals are able to calmly assess the situation, consider various solutions, and take decisive action. This proactive approach prevents you from feeling stuck or overwhelmed and empowers you to take control of your life.

Healthy relationships provide support and comfort during difficult times, making them a vital part of emotional resilience. Cultivating strong connections with family, friends, and colleagues creates a support network that can offer encouragement, advice, and practical help. In turn, offering support to others can reinforce your own resilience and foster a sense of community.

Self-care is an often overlooked but incredibly important aspect of emotional resilience. Regular physical activity, adequate sleep, nutritious eating, and engaging in hobbies and activities that bring you joy are all ways to take care of your physical and mental health. When you feel good physically, you're better equipped to handle emotional stress.

Finally, **optimism** and a **positive outlook** play a significant role in emotional resilience. This doesn't mean ignoring reality or pretending everything is fine when it's not. Rather, it's about maintaining a hopeful attitude and focusing on solutions rather than dwelling on problems. It involves trusting in your ability to overcome obstacles and viewing challenges as opportunities for growth.

To enhance your emotional resilience, consider incorporating some of the following strategies into your daily routine:

1. **Practice mindfulness** to increase self-awareness and reduce stress.

2. **Adopt a flexible mindset** to better adapt to change and uncertainty.

3. **Develop strong problem-solving skills** by approaching challenges with a clear, calm mind.

4. **Invest in relationships** that offer mutual support and understanding.

5. **Prioritize self-care** to maintain your physical and mental health.

6. **Cultivate optimism** by focusing on positive outcomes and learning from setbacks.

By actively working on these areas, you can strengthen your emotional resilience and enhance your ability to navigate life's challenges with confidence and poise.

Recognizing Emotional Triggers

Recognizing emotional triggers is a pivotal step in cultivating emotional resilience. It requires a deep dive into self-awareness, where you become an observer of your own mind and reactions. Emotional triggers can be as varied as the individuals experiencing them, ranging from specific words, situations, to even tones of voice that evoke a strong emotional response. These triggers often stem from past experiences, unresolved issues, or deeply held beliefs about ourselves and the world around us. By identifying these triggers, you empower yourself to manage your reactions more effectively, reducing the likelihood of being overwhelmed by negative emotions.

The first step in recognizing your emotional triggers is to maintain a daily log of your emotional responses. When you feel a strong emotion, take a moment to jot down the context, the thoughts running through your mind, and any physical sensations you experience. Over time, patterns will emerge, offering clues to your triggers. This exercise isn't about judgment but about understanding and acknowledging your emotional landscape.

Another strategy involves reflecting on instances where your reactions were more intense than the situation warranted. These disproportionate reactions are often red flags, indicating underlying emotional triggers. Ask yourself what about the situation felt threatening or deeply uncomfortable. Was it a fear of rejection, a sense of inadequacy, or perhaps a feeling of not being heard? Unpacking these moments can provide significant insights into your emotional triggers.

Mindfulness meditation is a powerful tool in this endeavor. It teaches you to stay present with your emotions, observing them without attachment. Through regular practice, you'll learn to notice the rise of emotions without immediately reacting, giving you the space to identify the trigger before it fully takes hold. This space is where resilience begins to grow, as you learn not only to recognize your triggers but also to understand that you have a choice in how to respond to them.

Engaging in open conversations with trusted individuals about your triggers and emotional responses can also be enlightening. Sometimes, an outside perspective can offer insights that are hard to see from within our own thought patterns. These discussions can also reinforce your support network, reminding you that you're not alone in your quest for emotional resilience.

Exploring your past, with or without the assistance of a professional, can shed light on the origins of your triggers. Many triggers are rooted in past traumas or significant life events. Understanding the source can sometimes diminish the power of the trigger, as it brings into consciousness what was previously operating in the shadows of your psyche.

Incorporating these strategies into your life doesn't mean that you'll never be triggered again or that you should aim for such an unrealistic goal. Instead, the objective is to become more aware of your triggers, reducing their ability to control your emotional responses. This awareness is a crucial component of emotional resilience, allowing you to navigate life's ups and downs with greater ease and stability.

As you become more adept at recognizing your emotional triggers, you'll find yourself responding to situations with increased calmness and clarity. This doesn't eliminate the complexity of human emotions but provides you with tools to manage them more effectively. Remember, the goal is not to suppress or ignore your emotions but to understand them deeply, creating a rich tapestry of self-awareness that supports your journey toward emotional resilience.

Building a Resilient Mindset

Cultivating a resilient mindset is akin to constructing a fortress within ourselves, one that stands steadfast against the adversities of life. This fortification does not arise from a denial of vulnerability but rather from the acknowledgment and embrace of our intrinsic strength and adaptability. To build this mindset, one must engage in practices that foster resilience, turning them into habitual responses that can weather life's storms.

One such practice is the cultivation of a positive self-dialogue. The language we use with ourselves, both internally and through spoken word, has a profound impact on our resilience. Negative self-talk reinforces feelings of helplessness and despair, while positive self-talk can uplift and empower. Start by becoming aware of the tone and content of your internal conversations. When you catch yourself spiraling into negativity, pause and reframe your thoughts. Replace critical or defeatist thoughts with affirmations of your strength, adaptability, and worth. This doesn't mean ignoring reality but choosing to focus on your capabilities and potential for growth.

Another cornerstone in building a resilient mindset is embracing failure as a stepping stone to success. Resilient individuals view setbacks not as insurmountable obstacles but as valuable learning experiences. When faced with failure, take the time to reflect on what went wrong and why. This reflection is not about assigning blame but about understanding and learning. Ask yourself, "What can I learn from this experience? How can I grow from this?" By adopting this perspective, every setback becomes an opportunity to build resilience and move closer to your goals.

Additionally, fostering a sense of purpose can significantly enhance your resilience. Purpose acts as a compass, guiding you through life's challenges and providing a sense of meaning that sustains motivation.

To discover your purpose, consider what you are passionate about, what skills you have to offer, and how you can contribute to something larger than yourself. Your purpose need not be grandiose; it simply needs to be meaningful to you. Once identified, align your actions and decisions with this purpose, allowing it to propel you forward even in the face of adversity.

Building resilience also involves cultivating strong, supportive relationships. Humans are inherently social beings, and our connections with others play a crucial role in our ability to cope with stress and bounce back from hardship. Invest time and energy in relationships that uplift and support you. Seek out individuals who encourage your growth and offer empathy and understanding. In turn, be a source of support for others, as giving support can be just as beneficial as receiving it. These reciprocal relationships create a network of resilience, amplifying your own and contributing to a community of strength.

Finally, maintaining physical health is a vital component of a resilient mindset. Regular exercise, adequate sleep, and a nutritious diet all contribute to our physical well-being, which in turn supports our mental and emotional resilience. Physical activity, in particular, is a powerful stress reliever and mood booster. Find an activity you enjoy, whether it's walking, cycling, yoga, or dancing, and make it a regular part of your routine. Prioritize sleep as a non-negotiable element of your day, and nourish your body with foods that fuel your energy and vitality.

In integrating these practices into your daily life, remember that building a resilient mindset is a gradual process. It requires patience, persistence, and a willingness to confront and grow from life's challenges.

Each step forward, no matter how small, is a victory in the journey of cultivating resilience. By committing to this path, you empower yourself to navigate life's ups and downs with grace, strength, and an unwavering belief in your ability to overcome.

Exercise n.13: Trigger Identification Journal Exercise

Objective: Build awareness and develop resilience by documenting common emotional triggers.

Type: Reflection Exercise

Duration: Daily, for at least 2 weeks.

Instructions:

Set Aside Time: Dedicate 10-15 minutes each day for this exercise. Consistency is key, so try to do it at the same time each day.

Find a Quiet Space: Choose a place where you won't be disturbed.

Daily Reflection Prompts: Answer the following prompts each day:

- *Identify Emotional Triggers*: Reflect on your day and write down any situations or interactions that triggered a strong emotional response. Be specific about what happened and how you felt.
- *Describe the Context*: Describe the context or situation in which the trigger occurred. What were you doing? Who were you with? What was happening around you?
- *Emotional Impact*: Reflect on the emotions you experienced. Did you feel anger, sadness, anxiety, frustration, or another emotion? Note the intensity of the emotion.
- *Behavioral Response*: Note any actions or behaviors that resulted from the emotional trigger. Did you react in a certain way? How did it affect your interactions or decisions?
- *Reflection and Insight*: Reflect on why this situation or interaction triggered you. Consider any underlying beliefs, past experiences, or patterns that may have contributed to your reaction.
- *Developing Resilience*: Identify strategies to manage and cope with similar triggers in the future. What can you do to build resilience and respond more calmly?

Weekly Review: At the end of each week, review your journal entries. Reflect on any patterns you notice and write a summary of your observations and any progress you've made in managing your triggers.

Consistency: Make this trigger identification journal exercise a non-negotiable part of your daily routine to foster emotional awareness and resilience.

Managing Stress and Anxiety Tools

Managing stress and anxiety effectively requires a toolkit of strategies that can be adapted to suit individual needs and situations. One fundamental tool is **deep breathing exercises**, which can quickly reduce stress levels by activating the body's relaxation response. Techniques such as the 4-7-8 method, where you breathe in for four seconds, hold for seven, and exhale for eight, can be particularly effective. **Progressive muscle relaxation** is another technique that involves tensing and then slowly relaxing each muscle group in the body, promoting physical and mental calmness.

Regular physical activity is a powerful stress reducer. Exercise not only improves physical health but also increases the production of endorphins, the brain's feel-good neurotransmitters. This doesn't mean you need to engage in intense workouts. Even a daily walk or a short yoga session can make a significant difference. **Mindfulness and meditation** practices are also invaluable tools. These practices help anchor thoughts in the present moment, reducing the tendency to ruminate on past events or worry about the future. Apps and online resources can provide guided meditations tailored to stress reduction.

Setting realistic goals and breaking tasks into manageable steps can prevent feeling overwhelmed. It's important to recognize and accept personal limits, setting boundaries to avoid overcommitting. **Time management techniques**, such as prioritizing tasks and using a planner, can help reduce anxiety related to deadlines and workload.

Establishing a support network is crucial. Sharing thoughts and concerns with trusted friends, family members, or a support group can provide emotional relief and practical advice. Sometimes, just knowing you're not alone in your feelings can be incredibly comforting. **Seeking professional help** when stress and anxiety become unmanageable is a sign of strength, not weakness. Therapists and counselors can offer strategies and perspectives that might not be apparent from within the situation.

Journaling is a simple yet effective tool for managing stress and anxiety. Writing down thoughts and feelings can provide an outlet for expressing what might be hard to say out loud. It can also help identify patterns in thoughts and triggers for anxiety, providing insights into how to manage these triggers more effectively. **Creating a routine** that includes time for relaxation and activities you enjoy can also be a protective factor against stress. Whether it's reading, gardening, or engaging in a hobby, taking time for leisure activities can provide a much-needed break from stressors.

Limiting intake of caffeine and sugar can help keep anxiety in check, as both can exacerbate feelings of nervousness and jitteriness. Ensuring a healthy, balanced diet and getting adequate sleep are foundational aspects of managing stress and anxiety. Sleep deprivation can significantly worsen the symptoms of anxiety, making it harder to cope with daily stressors.

Lastly, **practicing gratitude** can shift the focus from stressors to what is positive in life. Keeping a gratitude journal or simply reflecting on a few positive things at the end of each day can enhance overall well-being and resilience against stress.

By incorporating these tools and strategies into daily life, individuals can build a comprehensive approach to managing stress and anxiety. It's important to remember that what works for one person may not work for another, so it's beneficial to experiment with different techniques to find what best suits your needs.

Breathing and Mindfulness Techniques

Breathing and mindfulness techniques stand as powerful tools for managing stress and anxiety, offering a pathway to greater emotional resilience. These practices are rooted in the principle that by focusing on the present moment and regulating our breathing, we can exert control over our stress response, fostering a sense of calm and stability in the face of life's challenges.

Starting with breathing techniques, the practice of deep, diaphragmatic breathing is a cornerstone of stress reduction. This involves breathing deeply into the belly rather than shallow breaths into the chest, which can help trigger the body's relaxation response, slowing down the heart rate and lowering blood pressure. A simple exercise to begin with is the 4-7-8 technique, where you inhale deeply through your nose for 4 seconds, hold the breath for 7 seconds, and exhale slowly through the mouth for 8 seconds. This method not only helps in calming the mind but also in bringing one's focus back to the present.

Mindfulness, on the other hand, involves paying attention to the present moment without judgment. It can be practiced through mindfulness meditation, where the focus is on being acutely aware of what you're sensing and feeling in the moment, without interpretation or judgment. This can include paying attention to your breath, noticing the sensations in your body, or being aware of the thoughts that pass through your mind. Mindfulness meditation does not require any special equipment or environment – it can be practiced anywhere, whether you're sitting in a quiet room or taking a walk outside. The key is to bring your focus back to the present moment whenever you notice your mind wandering.

Incorporating these practices into your daily routine can start with just a few minutes each day and gradually increase as you become more comfortable with the techniques. Morning can be an ideal time to practice breathing exercises to set a calm tone for the day ahead, while mindfulness meditation can be a soothing way to unwind in the evening. However, the flexibility of these practices means they can be adapted to fit into any schedule or situation, offering a readily accessible tool to manage stress and enhance emotional resilience.

By engaging regularly with breathing and mindfulness techniques, you can develop a greater awareness of your emotional state, recognize stressors more readily, and respond to them more effectively. Over time, these practices can lead to lasting changes in how you relate to stress and anxiety, fostering a more resilient mindset that can navigate life's ups and downs with greater ease and stability. Through this intentional focus on the present and regulation of the breath, you can unlock a powerful means of cultivating inner strength and emotional resilience, laying the foundation for a more empowered and centered life.

Exercise n.14: Deep Breathing Practice Exercise

Objective: Manage stress and enhance resilience through a simple breathing Mindfulness exercise.
Duration: Daily, for at least 5-10 minutes.

Instructions:
Set Aside Time: Dedicate 5-10 minutes each day for this exercise. Consistency is key, so try to do it at the same time each day.

Find a Quiet Space: Choose a calm and comfortable place where you won't be disturbed.

Daily Practice: Follow these steps each day:
- *Get Comfortable*: Sit or lie down in a comfortable position. Close your eyes if it feels comfortable.
- *Focus on Your Breath*: Begin by taking a few breaths. How do you sense air entering and leaving your body?
- *Deep Breathing Technique*:
  - Inhale deeply through your nose for a count of four, allowing your abdomen to expand.
  - Hold your breath for a count of four.
  - Exhale slowly through your mouth for a count of six, allowing your abdomen to contract.
  - Pause for a count of two before taking your next breath.
- *Repeat the Cycle*: Continue this deep breathing cycle (inhale, hold, exhale, pause) for at least 5-10 minutes.
- *Stay Present*: Focus your attention on your breath rhythm. If your mind wanders, gently bring your focus back to your breathing.

Daily Reflection:
After practice note changes in stress, mood, or sensations.

Weekly Review: At the end of each week, review your reflections. Write a summary of your observations and any progress you've made in managing stress and enhancing resilience.

Consistency: Make this deep breathing practice a non-negotiable part of your daily routine to effectively manage stress and build resilience.

Self-Compassion and Kindness Practices

Building on the foundation of breathing and mindfulness techniques to manage stress and anxiety, the practice of **self-compassion and kindness** emerges as a vital component in cultivating emotional resilience. At its core, self-compassion involves treating oneself with the same kindness, concern, and support one would show to a good friend when facing difficult times. This concept, though simple, can be transformative, especially in a society that often emphasizes self-criticism and relentless self-improvement. By adopting self-compassion practices, individuals can create a nurturing inner dialogue that fosters emotional healing and resilience.

One effective method to cultivate self-compassion is through the practice of **mindful self-compassion (MSC)** exercises. These exercises encourage individuals to acknowledge their suffering, recognize that suffering is a part of the shared human experience, and extend kindness to themselves. For instance, when confronted with personal failings or challenges, instead of succumbing to harsh self-criticism, one might gently remind oneself, "This is a moment of suffering, suffering is part of life, may I be kind to myself in this moment, may I give myself the compassion I need." This simple yet profound practice can be a first step towards developing a more compassionate and supportive relationship with oneself.

Another powerful practice is to write **self-compassion letters** to oneself. During moments of self-doubt or criticism, taking the time to write a letter to oneself from the perspective of a compassionate friend can be incredibly healing. This exercise allows individuals to express understanding, validation, and encouragement to themselves, offering a tangible reminder of their inherent worth and the universality of their experiences.

Engaging in **kindness meditation** is also a beneficial practice. This form of meditation focuses on generating feelings of warmth and kindness towards oneself and others. Starting with directing kind thoughts to oneself, such as "May I be happy, may I be healthy, may I live with ease," and gradually extending these wishes to loved ones, acquaintances, and even those with whom one may have difficulties, can significantly enhance one's capacity for compassion and emotional resilience.

It is also crucial to recognize the role of **self-care** as an act of self-compassion. Regularly engaging in activities that nourish both the body and mind, whether it be through exercise, hobbies, or relaxation techniques, reinforces the importance of treating oneself with care and respect. Viewing self-care as a priority rather than a luxury can shift one's perspective towards self-compassion, emphasizing the value of one's well-being.

Lastly, **fostering a supportive community** that values self-compassion can amplify the benefits of these practices. Surrounding oneself with individuals who embody and encourage self-compassion can provide a supportive environment that nurtures growth and resilience. Whether through support groups, workshops, or mindful communities, connecting with others on the journey towards self-compassion can offer encouragement, inspiration, and a sense of belonging.

By integrating self-compassion and kindness practices into daily life, individuals can significantly enhance their emotional resilience. These practices not only offer immediate relief from the harshness of self-criticism but also foster a long-term transformation towards living a more compassionate, resilient, and fulfilled life. Engaging with these practices allows for the development of a gentle strength that supports navigating life's challenges with grace and ease, underscoring the profound impact of self-compassion on emotional health and well-being.

Exercise n.15: Self-Compassion Journal Exercise

Objective: Foster self-compassion and celebrate small accomplishments.
Type: Reflection and Kindness Exercise
Duration: Daily, for 10-15 minutes.

Instructions:
Set Aside Time: Dedicate 10-15 minutes each day.

Find a Quiet Space: Choose a calm and comfortable place.

Daily Reflection Prompts: Answer the following prompts each day:
- *Acknowledge Feelings*: Write down any difficult emotions or challenges you experienced during the day. Acknowledge these feelings without judgment.
- *Practice Self-Compassion*: Reflect on how you can be kind to yourself in response to these emotions or challenges. Write a compassionate statement to yourself as if you were comforting a friend.
- *Celebrate Small Wins*: List at least three small accomplishments or positive things that happened during the day. Celebrate these moments, no matter how minor they may seem.
- *Gratitude Reflection*: Write down three things you are grateful for. This helps shift your focus to the positive aspects of your life.

Document Your Reflections: At the end of each week, review your journal entries. Reflect on any patterns you notice and write a summary of your observations and any progress you've made in fostering self-compassion.

Consistency: Make this self-compassion journal exercise a non-negotiable part of your daily routine to foster kindness towards yourself and celebrate your accomplishments.

Overcoming Obstacles with a Growth Mindset

Adopting a growth mindset is essential in transforming obstacles into stepping stones for personal development. This mindset, characterized by the belief that abilities and intelligence can be developed through dedication and hard work, offers a powerful framework for overcoming challenges. It encourages seeing failures not as evidence of unintelligence but as opportunities for growth and learning.

Embrace failures as learning opportunities: Every setback or failure is a chance to learn. Instead of viewing them as a reflection of your capabilities, see them as valuable feedback on your journey. Analyze what went wrong, adjust your strategies, and try again with a better understanding.

Cultivate curiosity: Approach challenges with a sense of curiosity. Ask questions, seek out new information, and explore different strategies. This can transform a daunting obstacle into an interesting problem to solve, making the process of overcoming it more engaging and less intimidating.

Focus on effort, not talent: Recognize that effort is the key to mastering new skills. Praising effort rather than innate talent encourages persistence in the face of challenges. It reinforces the idea that you can improve through hard work and dedication.

Celebrate progress, no matter how small: Acknowledge and celebrate every small win or progress. This reinforces the value of your efforts and keeps motivation high. Recognizing incremental achievements helps maintain a positive outlook, even when the end goal seems far away.

Seek feedback and use it constructively: Feedback, even when it's critical, is invaluable for growth. Seek out feedback actively and use it constructively to make adjustments and improvements. Viewing feedback as a gift rather than a criticism can change how you approach challenges.

Develop resilience through positive affirmations: Positive affirmations can bolster your resilience. Remind yourself of your ability to grow and learn, especially in moments of doubt. Phrases like "I am capable of learning and growing" or "Each step forward makes me stronger" can be powerful motivators.

Surround yourself with a supportive community: Being part of a community that values growth and learning can significantly impact your ability to overcome obstacles. Engage with mentors, peers, or groups who encourage a growth mindset and offer support and encouragement.

Reflect on past successes: When faced with a new challenge, reflect on past instances where you've overcome obstacles. This reflection can boost your confidence and remind you that you are capable of tackling challenges and emerging stronger.

By integrating these practices into your daily life, you can harness the power of a growth mindset to overcome obstacles. This approach not only facilitates personal growth but also contributes to a more fulfilling and resilient life. Engaging with challenges from a place of growth and learning can transform the way you perceive obstacles, turning them into opportunities for development and self-improvement.

Embracing Challenges for Growth

Facing challenges head-on and perceiving them as opportunities for growth rather than insurmountable obstacles is a mindset shift that can significantly impact one's journey towards emotional resilience and inner strength. This perspective encourages a proactive approach to problem-solving and personal development, where each challenge becomes a stepping stone towards greater understanding and self-improvement. By adopting this approach, individuals can foster a resilient mindset that thrives on the lessons learned from each experience, no matter how difficult it may seem at the outset. One practical way to embrace challenges as learning opportunities is by maintaining a reflective journal dedicated to personal growth and resilience. In this journal, document each challenge faced, the emotions it evoked, the strategies employed to overcome it, and most importantly, the lessons learned. This practice not only serves as a record of personal growth but also as a reminder of the individual's ability to navigate through tough times. It's a tangible proof of the progress made and the resilience built over time. Another method involves actively seeking out new challenges that push you slightly out of your comfort zone. This could be learning a new skill, taking on a project that requires a new level of expertise, or even engaging in activities that test your physical limits. The key is to approach these challenges with a mindset focused on learning and growth, rather than perfection or fear of failure. Embrace the discomfort that comes with being a beginner and celebrate the small victories along the way. Furthermore, cultivating a network of support plays a crucial role in transforming challenges into opportunities for growth. Surround yourself with individuals who not only support your goals but also challenge you to stretch beyond your current capabilities. This supportive community can provide valuable feedback, encouragement, and different perspectives that can help you navigate through challenges more effectively. Engaging in meaningful conversations about failures, setbacks, and successes within this network can inspire new strategies for personal and professional growth. Additionally, adopting a practice of regular self-reflection can enhance your ability to see challenges as opportunities. Set aside time to reflect on your experiences, the outcomes of your efforts, and the growth that resulted from each challenge. Ask yourself what you would do differently next time, what skills you need to develop further, and how you can apply the lessons learned in future situations. This practice not only deepens your self-awareness but also reinforces the growth mindset that views challenges as essential for learning and development. Lastly, it's important to recognize the role of resilience training in preparing oneself to face challenges head-on. Engage in activities that build emotional resilience, such as mindfulness meditation, stress management techniques, and exercises that enhance adaptability. These practices not only equip you with the tools needed to manage stress and anxiety but also strengthen your capacity to recover from setbacks more quickly. By integrating these strategies into your daily life, you can cultivate a mindset that not only embraces challenges as learning opportunities but also celebrates the growth and resilience that come from navigating through them. This approach not only contributes to personal and professional development but also to the cultivation of a fulfilling and empowered life where challenges are viewed not as barriers but as catalysts for growth and transformation.

Developing Confidence Through Small Wins

Harnessing the power of small wins is a transformative strategy for building confidence. This approach centers on setting and achieving micro-goals, which, though seemingly minor, cumulate significant positive impacts on one's self-esteem and overall emotional resilience. Each small win acts as a stepping stone, gradually constructing a robust foundation of confidence that supports larger goals and more complex challenges. The beauty of small wins lies in their accessibility; they do not require monumental effort or drastic changes to one's lifestyle. Instead, they integrate seamlessly into daily routines, offering consistent opportunities for success and the reinforcement of a growth mindset.

To effectively develop confidence through small wins, start by identifying areas in your life where you seek improvement or wish to build greater competence. This could range from personal development goals, such as cultivating a habit of daily meditation, to professional aspirations like enhancing public speaking skills. Once these areas are identified, break down the larger goal into smaller, manageable tasks that can be tackled on a daily or weekly basis. For instance, if the goal is to improve public speaking, a small win could be practicing a speech in front of a mirror or recording oneself to critique later. These tasks should be specific, measurable, achievable, relevant, and time-bound (SMART), ensuring that each small win is clearly defined and attainable within a set timeframe.

Celebrating these small victories is crucial. Acknowledgment and reward reinforce the positive behavior and bolster one's motivation to continue pursuing further goals. Celebration does not necessarily mean grand gestures; it can be as simple as taking a moment to reflect on the achievement, sharing the success with a friend, or treating oneself to a favorite activity. The act of celebration, regardless of its form, serves as a powerful reminder of one's capability and progress, further embedding the confidence gained from each small win.

Moreover, tracking progress is an essential aspect of this strategy. Maintaining a journal or log where you can record each small win provides tangible evidence of your achievements and the cumulative growth over time. This record not only serves as a motivational tool but also helps in identifying patterns or areas where adjustments may be needed. It's a practice that reinforces the growth mindset, encouraging a focus on progress and learning rather than perfection or the avoidance of failure.

Incorporating feedback into the process of achieving small wins is another vital component. Constructive feedback, whether from oneself or others, offers insights into how to adjust and improve strategies for achieving these micro-goals. It's an opportunity for learning and growth, fostering a resilient and adaptable approach to personal and professional development.

Lastly, it's important to leverage the support of a community or network. Sharing goals and celebrating small wins with others can amplify the sense of achievement and provide a source of encouragement and accountability. Whether it's through social media, a personal blog, or a support group, connecting with others on a similar journey can enhance the experience and effectiveness of building confidence through small wins.

By focusing on small wins, individuals can gradually build a strong sense of self-efficacy and confidence. This approach not only makes goals more attainable but also transforms the process of personal growth into a more enjoyable and rewarding journey. Through the accumulation of small wins, one can develop the resilience and confidence needed to tackle larger challenges and achieve greater successes, embodying the essence of cultivating emotional resilience and embracing a growth mindset.

Exercise n.16: Small Wins Tracker Exercise

Objective: Build confidence and a growth mindset by tracking small daily victories.
Type: Progress Tracking Exercise
Duration: Daily, for at least 10 minutes.

Instructions:
Set Aside Time: Dedicate 10 minutes each day for this exercise. Consistency is key, so try to do it at the same time each day.

Find a Quiet Space: Choose a calm and comfortable place where you won't be disturbed.

Daily Reflection Prompts: Answer the following prompts each day:
* *Identify Small Wins*: Reflect on your day and write down at least three small victories or positive actions you took. These can be minor achievements or moments of progress.
* *Describe the Impact*: Describe how each small win made you feel and the positive impact it had on your day. Consider how these wins contribute to your overall goals and well-being.
* *Acknowledge Effort*: Recognize the effort you put into achieving these small wins. Write a brief note of self-appreciation for your hard work and dedication.

Weekly Review: At the end of each week, review your tracker. Reflect on any patterns you notice and write a summary of your observations and any progress you've made in building confidence and a growth mindset.

Consistency: Make this small wins tracker exercise a non-negotiable part of your daily routine to foster a sense of accomplishment and continuous improvement.

Building Authentic Relationships

Authentic relationships, the cornerstone of a fulfilling life, require more than just surface-level interactions; they demand vulnerability, honesty, and a deep sense of trust. The foundation of such relationships is built on the willingness to be open about one's feelings, desires, and fears. This openness paves the way for genuine connections, where both parties feel seen, heard, and valued. To cultivate these meaningful relationships, it's crucial to start with self-awareness. Understanding your own emotions, triggers, and communication styles can significantly improve how you relate to others. It enables you to approach interactions with empathy and a clear understanding of your boundaries and needs.

Active listening plays a pivotal role in building authentic connections. It involves fully concentrating on what is being said rather than passively hearing the message of the speaker. Active listening means being present and engaged, offering non-verbal feedback, and reflecting on what has been said by paraphrasing or asking clarifying questions. This level of engagement shows the speaker they have your full attention and that you value their thoughts and feelings, fostering a deeper bond.

Another key aspect is the expression of appreciation and gratitude in relationships. Acknowledging and appreciating the qualities and efforts of those around you can reinforce positive interactions and mutual respect. Simple gestures of gratitude can strengthen bonds and ensure that relationships are nurturing and supportive. It's also essential to practice forgiveness and understanding. Holding onto grudges or dwelling on past conflicts can hinder the growth of a relationship. Approaching misunderstandings with a willingness to forgive and learn from the experience can open up avenues for deeper connection and trust.

Setting and respecting boundaries is equally important in maintaining healthy relationships. Clear boundaries help manage expectations and ensure that both parties feel respected and understood. It's about knowing where you end and the other person begins, recognizing that each individual's needs and comfort levels are valid and should be honored.

In the pursuit of authentic relationships, it's also vital to engage in shared experiences and activities that foster connection and joy. Whether it's exploring new hobbies, volunteering for a shared cause, or simply spending quality time together, these shared moments can deepen bonds and create lasting memories. Engaging in open and honest communication about one's feelings, aspirations, and concerns can further solidify the foundation of trust and understanding in a relationship.

Lastly, it's important to remember that building authentic relationships is a journey, not a destination. It requires continuous effort, patience, and a willingness to grow and adapt. By prioritizing honesty, empathy, and mutual respect, individuals can cultivate connections that are not only deeply fulfilling but also resilient in the face of life's challenges.

Embracing vulnerability is a powerful tool for deepening connections and fostering authenticity in relationships. It involves letting down your guard and sharing your true self, including your fears, dreams, and insecurities. This level of openness can be daunting, but it's essential for building trust and intimacy. When both parties in a relationship dare to be vulnerable, it creates a safe space for genuine understanding and connection. This mutual vulnerability acts as a catalyst for strengthening the bond, allowing individuals to truly see and accept each other for who they are, flaws and all.

Conflict resolution skills are crucial in maintaining authentic relationships. Disagreements and conflicts are natural in any relationship, but how they are handled can either strengthen or weaken the bond. Approaching conflicts with a mindset focused on finding a solution rather than winning an argument encourages open communication and compromise. It's important to listen actively, acknowledge the other person's perspective, and express your own feelings and needs in a respectful manner. This approach fosters a healthy environment where conflicts are resolved constructively, contributing to the relationship's growth and resilience.

Investing time and energy into relationships is another key aspect of building authenticity. Like any meaningful endeavor, relationships require effort and commitment. This means making time for each other, being present during interactions, and showing consistent interest and care. It's the small, everyday actions—sending a thoughtful message, remembering important dates, or simply asking how the other person's day was—that accumulate and reinforce the significance of the relationship. By prioritizing and nurturing these connections, individuals demonstrate their commitment and affection, further solidifying the bond.

Encouraging personal growth within the context of a relationship is also essential. Authentic relationships thrive on mutual support and encouragement towards personal development and self-discovery. Celebrating each other's successes, supporting each other through challenges, and inspiring one another to pursue goals and dreams can enhance the connection and provide a sense of partnership and teamwork. This shared journey of growth not only enriches the individual lives of those involved but also strengthens the relationship as a whole, creating a dynamic where both parties feel valued and empowered.

In conclusion, building authentic relationships is a multifaceted process that involves a combination of self-awareness, vulnerability, active listening, appreciation, conflict resolution, investment of time and energy, and support for personal growth. These elements work together to create a foundation of trust, understanding, and mutual respect, which are essential for deep, meaningful connections. By embracing these principles and committing to the continuous nurturing of relationships, individuals can forge bonds that are not only fulfilling but also enduring and resilient.

The Value of Connection

In the realm of **authentic relationships**, the value of connection transcends mere social interaction, becoming a cornerstone of personal growth and inner strength. It is through these genuine connections that individuals find the support, empathy, and mutual understanding necessary for navigating life's challenges. The essence of building authentic relationships lies not just in seeking companionship but in fostering deep, meaningful bonds that enrich our lives and nurture our personal development.

To cultivate these connections, it is imperative to practice **empathy** and **active listening**. Empathy allows us to understand and share the feelings of others, creating a safe space for vulnerability and openness. Active listening, on the other hand, involves fully concentrating on what is being said rather than passively hearing the message of the speaker. It's about listening with all senses and giving full attention to the speaker, which is crucial in strengthening relationships.

Another key aspect is the **practical exercise of relationship reflection**. This involves taking time to consider the state of our current relationships, identifying areas for improvement, and acknowledging the aspects that are thriving. By regularly reflecting on our relationships, we can become more intentional in how we engage with those around us, ensuring that our connections remain strong and authentic.

Creating **boundaries** is also essential in building and maintaining healthy relationships. Boundaries help protect our energy and ensure that our relationships are mutually respectful and beneficial. Learning to identify **healthy vs. toxic relationships** is crucial in this process. Healthy relationships are characterized by mutual respect, trust, and support, while toxic relationships drain energy and undermine self-esteem.

Boundary-setting techniques play a significant role in personal growth. They involve clear communication of one's needs and limits within relationships. Establishing and maintaining these boundaries can lead to more fulfilling and empowering connections.

In conclusion, understanding the value of connection in the context of building authentic relationships is about recognizing the profound impact that genuine, empathetic, and supportive interactions can have on our lives. It's about prioritizing quality over quantity, depth over surface-level engagements, and mutual growth over mere companionship. By embracing these principles, individuals can forge stronger bonds that not only withstand the test of time but also contribute significantly to their journey of personal empowerment and inner strength.

Why Authentic Relationships Matter

The significance of nurturing **authentic relationships** in our lives cannot be overstated, especially in a world where digital connections often overshadow face-to-face interactions. These genuine connections serve as a vital source of support, allowing us to experience a sense of belonging and understanding that is crucial for our emotional and psychological well-being. Authentic relationships offer a mirror through which we see ourselves reflected in the honesty, acceptance, and love of another person. This reflection not only reinforces our sense of identity but also encourages personal growth and self-discovery.

Engaging in deep, meaningful conversations rather than superficial exchanges fosters a sense of intimacy and trust, laying the foundation for relationships that can provide comfort and guidance during times of stress or uncertainty. These interactions are characterized by a mutual sharing of thoughts, feelings, and experiences, where both parties feel heard and valued. The strength of these connections often lies in their ability to withstand the challenges and adversities life throws our way, offering a safe harbor in the storm.

Moreover, authentic relationships contribute significantly to our ability to develop resilience. When we know we have a network of supportive relationships, we are more likely to bounce back from setbacks and face challenges with a greater sense of confidence and optimism. These relationships provide a sounding board for our fears and frustrations, as well as our hopes and dreams, allowing us to process our emotions in a healthy and constructive manner.

The act of building and maintaining these connections requires effort and intentionality. It involves showing up as our true selves, being vulnerable, and allowing others to see us as we are, flaws and all. This level of honesty and openness fosters a deep sense of trust and respect, which are the cornerstones of any lasting relationship. It also means being present, both physically and emotionally, for the people we care about, and investing time and energy into nurturing these bonds.

Practicing empathy and active listening, as mentioned earlier, is crucial in this process. It allows us to connect with others on a deeper level, to understand their perspectives and experiences, and to respond with compassion and kindness. These skills are not innate; they require practice and dedication to develop. However, the rewards of such efforts are immeasurable, leading to richer, more fulfilling relationships that enrich our lives in countless ways.

Furthermore, establishing and respecting boundaries is another key aspect of building authentic relationships. Healthy boundaries help ensure that our relationships are balanced and mutually beneficial, preventing resentment and burnout. They allow us to communicate our needs and limits clearly, fostering an environment of mutual respect and understanding.

As we continue to navigate the complexities of human relationships, it's important to remember that the quality of our connections matters far more than the quantity. In an age where social media often dictates the standards of social interaction, choosing to cultivate deep, meaningful relationships is a radical act of self-care and empowerment. It's through these authentic connections that we find the strength, support, and love necessary to face life's challenges and embrace our journey towards personal growth and fulfillment.

Connection vs. Surface-Level Interactions

In the landscape of human connections, the distinction between genuine interaction and mere surface-level engagement is profound. Surface-level interactions, often characterized by small talk or casual, fleeting exchanges, may serve a purpose in social niceties or brief encounters. However, they lack the depth and substance that forge lasting bonds and meaningful relationships. Authentic connections, on the other hand, are built on a foundation of deep, meaningful communication, shared experiences, and mutual respect and understanding. These are the relationships that not only endure but also provide a source of strength, comfort, and joy throughout the various seasons of life.

To move beyond the superficial and cultivate connections that truly matter, it's essential to be intentional about how we communicate and interact with others. This means taking the time to really listen to what others are saying, engaging in conversations with a genuine interest, and sharing our own thoughts and feelings openly and honestly. It's about being present in the moment, giving our full attention to the person we're with, rather than allowing distractions to pull us away. In a world where digital communication often takes precedence over face-to-face interactions, making a conscious effort to connect on a deeper level can feel challenging, yet it's more important than ever.

One practical step towards deepening connections is to create opportunities for meaningful interaction. This could involve setting aside regular times to catch up with friends or family members, engaging in activities together that foster a sense of camaraderie and shared purpose, or simply making a point to ask more thoughtful, open-ended questions that encourage a deeper dialogue. It's also important to show vulnerability, allowing others to see our true selves. This can help to break down barriers and build trust, creating a safe space where authentic relationships can flourish.

Moreover, recognizing and appreciating the value of these deeper connections can motivate us to invest the time and energy required to maintain them. In an age of fleeting interactions and transient connections, choosing to focus on relationships that offer real depth and meaning is a powerful statement about the kind of life we wish to lead. It's a commitment to quality over quantity, depth over breadth, and lasting significance over momentary satisfaction.

Building authentic relationships requires patience, effort, and a willingness to step out of our comfort zones. It's not always easy, and there may be times when it feels like we're not making progress. However, the rewards of such relationships are immeasurable. They provide a source of support, inspiration, and joy that is unparalleled, enriching our lives in countless ways. By prioritizing these genuine connections over surface-level interactions, we not only enhance our own well-being but also contribute to a more connected, compassionate world.

Therefore, the challenge lies not in avoiding superficial interactions altogether but in not allowing them to dominate our relationships. It's about making a conscious choice to seek out and nurture connections that bring out the best in us and others. As we do so, we'll find that our lives become richer, our hearts fuller, and our journeys through life more rewarding. The effort to move beyond the surface and connect on a deeper level is an investment in our happiness and fulfillment, one that promises returns far greater than we might initially imagine.

Exercise n.17: Relationship Reflection Exercise

Objective: Reflect on meaningful relationships and identify areas for strengthening connections.

Type: Reflection Exercise

Duration: Weekly, for at least 15-20 minutes.

Instructions:

Set Aside Time: Dedicate 15-20 minutes each week for this exercise. Consistency is key, so try to do it at the same time each week (e.g., Sunday evening).

Find a Quiet Space:
Choose a calm and comfortable place where you won't be disturbed.

Weekly Reflection Prompts: Answer the following prompts each week:

- *Identify Meaningful Relationships*: Write down the names of people who are significant to your life and why they matter.
- *Positive Interactions*: Recall and write down positive and joyful interactions you had with these individuals during the week.
- *Areas for Improvement*: Identify any areas where you feel the relationship could be strengthened.
- *Action Plan*: Outline specific actions you can take to strengthen these relationships. This could include reaching out more often, expressing appreciation, resolving conflicts, or spending quality time together.
- *Gratitude Reflection*: Write down three things you are grateful for in your relationships. This helps shift your focus to the positive aspects and reinforces appreciation.

Document Your Reflections: Use a notebook, a digital document, or a journaling app to record your weekly reflections. This will help you track your progress over time.

Consistency: Make this relationship reflection exercise a non-negotiable part of your weekly routine to foster deeper connections and improve your relationships.

Strengthening Key Relationships

To effectively strengthen key relationships, it's essential to engage in activities that nurture connection and understanding. Regularly scheduling quality time together, whether it's a weekly dinner date, a monthly hiking trip, or daily conversations without distractions, can significantly enhance the bond between individuals. During these times, focus on sharing experiences, thoughts, and feelings openly. This shared vulnerability fosters deeper emotional connections and mutual trust.

Another pivotal strategy is expressing appreciation and gratitude towards each other. Taking the time to acknowledge and verbalize what you value in the other person not only boosts their self-esteem but also reinforces your bond. Simple gestures of appreciation, such as leaving a heartfelt note or verbally expressing thanks for everyday efforts, can have profound effects on the health of the relationship.

Active listening plays a critical role in strengthening relationships. It involves giving your undivided attention to the speaker, refraining from formulating a response while the other person is talking. Instead, listen with empathy, trying to understand their perspective without judgment. This level of attentiveness communicates respect and care, making the other person feel valued and understood.

Conflict resolution skills are indispensable for maintaining strong relationships. Approach disagreements with a mindset geared towards finding a solution that respects both parties' needs and perspectives. Effective communication is key here; express your feelings and needs clearly and calmly, without placing blame. Seek to understand the other person's point of view and work together to find a compromise or solution that strengthens the relationship rather than weakening it.

Investing in personal growth and encouraging your partner or friend to do the same can also enhance your relationship. As individuals evolve and develop new interests, sharing these experiences can bring excitement and fresh energy into the relationship. Support each other's goals and dreams, offering encouragement and being each other's cheerleader.

Finally, practicing forgiveness is crucial. Holding onto grudges or resentment can erode the foundation of any relationship. Understand that everyone makes mistakes and that forgiveness is a powerful step towards healing and moving forward stronger.

By incorporating these strategies, individuals can significantly strengthen their key relationships, creating a foundation of trust, mutual respect, and deep, meaningful connection. These efforts not only enhance personal happiness and fulfillment but also contribute to a supportive network that fosters resilience and growth.

Practicing Empathy and Active Listening

Empathy and active listening are foundational skills that, when practiced diligently, can transform the quality of our relationships, making them more authentic and connected. Empathy allows us to step into the shoes of another person, to understand their feelings and perspectives without judgment. This compassionate understanding is crucial in building trust and closeness in any relationship. Active listening, on the other hand, is the art of fully concentrating on what is being said, rather than just passively 'hearing' the message of the speaker. It involves listening with all of one's senses and giving full attention to the speaker. This level of engagement shows the speaker that they are valued and understood, which is essential in strengthening the bonds between individuals.

To develop empathy, one effective strategy is to consciously remind oneself to view situations from the other person's perspective. This can be challenging, especially when personal biases and judgments cloud our understanding. However, by making a concerted effort to consider the feelings and motivations behind someone else's actions or words, we can begin to cultivate a deeper sense of empathy. It's about acknowledging that everyone has a unique story and set of experiences that shape their view of the world. Practicing empathy also means recognizing and validating the emotions of others, even if we don't necessarily agree with their perspective. This validation can be as simple as saying, "I can see why you would feel that way," or "It sounds like you're really going through a tough time."

Active listening involves several key components. Firstly, it requires giving the speaker your undivided attention. This might mean putting away electronic devices, making eye contact, and ensuring your body language is open and inviting. It also involves listening to understand, not to reply. Often, we listen with half an ear, already formulating our response before the other person has finished speaking. Active listening, however, means focusing fully on the speaker's words, tone of voice, and body language to gain a complete understanding of their message. It's also helpful to provide feedback by paraphrasing or summarizing what the speaker has said, which not only shows that you are paying attention but also clarifies any misunderstandings right away.

Additionally, asking open-ended questions can encourage the speaker to elaborate on their thoughts and feelings, providing a deeper insight into their perspective. These questions show that you are engaged and interested in what they have to say. Moreover, it's important to avoid interrupting or finishing the speaker's sentences, as this can make them feel undervalued and hinder open communication. Instead, allow them to express themselves fully before you respond.

Incorporating these practices into daily interactions can significantly enhance the quality of our relationships. It fosters an environment where all parties feel heard, understood, and respected, which is the bedrock of any strong and authentic relationship. While empathy and active listening may not come naturally to everyone, they are skills that can be developed over time with patience, practice, and a genuine desire to connect with others on a deeper level. As we become more adept at practicing empathy and active listening, we not only improve our personal relationships but also contribute to a more compassionate and understanding world. These skills enable us to navigate conflicts more effectively, build stronger emotional connections, and create a supportive network of relationships that can sustain us through life's challenges. They are indispensable tools in our journey toward building lasting, authentic connections, enriching our lives and the lives of those around us.

Exercise n.18: Active Listening Practice Exercise

Objective: Improve communication skills by practicing active listening with a close friend or family member.
Type: Practice Exercise
Duration: Weekly, for at least 20-30 minutes.

Instructions:
Choose a Partner: Select a close friend to participate in this exercise with you. Explain the purpose and benefits of active listening.

Set a Regular Meeting Time: Schedule a consistent time each week for your active listening practice. Choose a time that works well for both.

Find a Quiet Space: Choose a calm and comfortable place where you won't be disturbed during your conversation.

Active Listening Steps: Follow these steps during your conversation:
- Be Present: Give your full attention to your partner. Put away distractions such as phones or other devices.
- Show Interest: Use non-verbal cues to show you are listening, such as nodding, maintaining eye contact, and leaning slightly forward.
- Reflect and Paraphrase: Reflect on what your partner is saying and paraphrase their words to show understanding. For example, "What I hear you saying is..." or "It sounds like you're feeling..."
- Ask Open-Ended Questions: Encourage your partner to share more by asking open-ended questions such as "Can you tell me more about that?" or "How did that make you feel?"
- Avoid Interrupting: Wait until they have finished before responding.
- Validate Their Feelings: Acknowledge and validate your partner's emotions. For example, "I can see why you would feel that way" or "That sounds really challenging."

Post-Conversation Reflection: After the conversation, take a moment to reflect on what you did well and any areas for improvement.

Document Your Reflections: Write down your reflections. This will help you track your progress over time.

Consistency: Ensure to practice this routine once per week to improve your communication skills and strengthen your relationships.

Exercise n.19: Gratitude for Relationships Exercise

Objective: Foster appreciation and strengthen connections by writing down qualities you appreciate in loved ones.

Type: Gratitude Exercise

Duration: Weekly, for at least 10-15 minutes.

Instructions:

Set Aside Time: Dedicate 10-15 minutes each week for this exercise. Consistency is key, so try to do it at the same time each week (e.g., Sunday evening).

Find a Quiet Space: Choose a calm and comfortable place where you won't be disturbed.

Weekly Reflection Prompts: Answer the following prompts each week:

- Identify Loved Ones: Reflect on the important people in your life. Write down the names of a few loved ones you want to focus on this week.
- Appreciate Qualities: For each person, write down at least three qualities or actions you appreciate about them. Be specific about what you value and why it matters to you.
- Reflect on Impact: Reflect on how these qualities or actions positively impact your life and your relationship with each person.
- Express Gratitude: Consider expressing your gratitude to these loved ones. This could be through a heartfelt conversation, a written note, or a small gesture of appreciation.

Document Your Reflections: Use a notebook, a digital document, or a journaling app to record your weekly reflections. This will help you track your appreciation over time and deepen your relationships.

Consistency: Make this gratitude for relationships exercise a non-negotiable part of your weekly routine to foster a greater sense of appreciation and strengthen your connections.

Creating Boundaries, Protecting Energy

Creating boundaries is an essential step in protecting your energy and ensuring that your relationships are healthy and supportive. This process involves defining what is acceptable and unacceptable in your interactions with others, which can significantly impact your emotional well-being and personal growth. It's about knowing where you end and someone else begins, recognizing that your needs, feelings, and interests are valid and deserve respect. To effectively establish boundaries, start by **identifying your limits**. Understand your emotional, physical, and mental thresholds. Reflect on past experiences where you felt discomfort, resentment, or frustration in your relationships. These feelings often signal that a boundary has been crossed. Once you have a clear understanding of your limits, **communicate them clearly** to others. Use "I" statements to express your needs and feelings without blaming or accusing others. For example, say, "I feel overwhelmed when we don't plan our family visits ahead of time. I need us to agree on a schedule that works for both of us."

Practicing assertiveness is key in boundary setting. Being assertive means expressing your thoughts, feelings, and needs in an open and honest way, while also respecting the rights and beliefs of others. It's not about being aggressive or passive but finding a healthy balance that allows you to stand up for yourself. **Seek mutual respect** in your relationships. Boundaries are not about controlling others but about managing your own actions and reactions. Encourage a reciprocal understanding where both parties' boundaries are acknowledged and respected.

Setting boundaries with technology is also crucial in today's digital age. Be intentional about how you use social media and communicate via digital platforms. Determine specific times when you will not check your email or social media to give yourself a break from the constant connectivity. **Learn to say no**. Saying no is a powerful tool in maintaining your boundaries. It allows you to honor your needs and limits without overcommitting or feeling overwhelmed. Remember, saying no doesn't mean you are selfish; it means you are taking care of yourself.

Enforcing your boundaries is perhaps the most challenging part. It requires consistency and the willingness to address violations when they occur. If someone disregards your boundaries, communicate the issue promptly and reinforce your expectations. It might feel uncomfortable at first, but it is crucial for your well-being. **Adjust and renegotiate boundaries as needed**. As you grow and your circumstances change, your boundaries might need to evolve. Regularly revisiting and adjusting your boundaries ensures they remain relevant and effective.

Engage in self-reflection to understand your progress in setting and maintaining boundaries. Reflect on situations where you successfully upheld your boundaries and instances where you struggled. Consider what worked, what didn't, and what you can do differently next time. **Seek support** if you find it difficult to establish or maintain boundaries. Talk to friends, family, or a professional who can offer guidance and encouragement. Remember, setting boundaries is a skill that takes practice and patience to develop. It's an ongoing process that plays a critical role in fostering authentic relationships and protecting your energy. By taking these steps, you empower yourself to build connections that are respectful, supportive, and fulfilling.

Healthy vs. Toxic Relationships

Identifying the distinction between healthy and toxic relationships is pivotal for protecting your energy and ensuring your interactions contribute positively to your inner strength and overall well-being. Healthy relationships are characterized by mutual respect, support, open communication, and the freedom to be oneself without fear of judgment or retribution. These relationships bolster your sense of self-worth and empower you to pursue personal growth and happiness. On the other hand, toxic relationships drain your energy, often making you feel trapped, undervalued, and constantly on edge. They can manifest through patterns of manipulation, disrespect, and lack of empathy, which are detrimental to your mental and emotional health.

To navigate through the complexities of your relationships, start by evaluating the dynamics present. Are your thoughts and feelings valued? Do you feel an equitable exchange of support and understanding? Healthy relationships thrive on reciprocity and balance, where both individuals feel seen and heard. If you notice recurring patterns of neglect, control, or emotional abuse, these are red flags signaling a toxic dynamic.

Creating boundaries is a crucial step in managing or exiting toxic relationships. Articulate your needs and limits clearly and assertively. Remember, setting boundaries is not an act of selfishness; it's a profound act of self-respect. It teaches others how to treat you and signals what you will and will not tolerate. In instances where boundaries are repeatedly disrespected, it may be necessary to reconsider the role of these relationships in your life.

Fostering healthy relationships begins with self-awareness and a commitment to personal growth. Cultivate qualities within yourself that you seek in others, such as empathy, honesty, and respect. By embodying these traits, you attract like-minded individuals who resonate with your values and contribute positively to your journey of building inner strength.

Moreover, investing time and energy into relationships that encourage mutual growth, understanding, and respect is essential for nurturing a supportive network. These relationships become a source of strength and comfort during challenging times, reinforcing your resilience and capacity for emotional balance.

In summary, by identifying and understanding the dynamics of healthy versus toxic relationships, you equip yourself with the knowledge to cultivate connections that enrich your life. This not only enhances your personal growth and happiness but also fortifies your inner strength, enabling you to navigate life's ups and downs with greater ease and confidence.

Boundary-Setting for Personal Growth

Effective boundary-setting is an essential skill for fostering personal growth and nurturing authentic relationships. It involves communicating your needs and limits clearly and respectfully, without fear of backlash or guilt. This process begins with self-reflection, understanding what you truly value and require from your interactions with others. Recognize that your needs are valid and that you have the right to express them. Start by identifying areas in your life where boundaries are lacking or not respected. This might include your time, energy, emotional space, or physical boundaries. Once these areas are identified, consider the specific changes that need to occur to protect these boundaries.

Articulating your boundaries to others is the next critical step. Use "I" statements to express your needs and feelings without placing blame or making the other person defensive. For example, instead of saying, "You always disregard my feelings," try, "I feel overwhelmed when my feelings are not considered, and I need our conversations to acknowledge both of our perspectives." This approach fosters open communication and mutual respect. Remember, it's not just about setting boundaries but also about responding to them being crossed. Have a plan for how you will address boundary violations. This might involve a conversation to reiterate your needs, taking a step back from the relationship, or seeking external support if the situation does not improve.

Implementing boundaries with kindness and consistency is crucial. People may initially react negatively to your boundaries, especially if they are not used to them. However, consistency in enforcing your boundaries teaches others how to treat you and demonstrates your commitment to your well-being. It's also important to respect the boundaries of others, as this sets a foundation for mutual respect and understanding in your relationships.

Practicing boundary-setting also means being flexible. Life is dynamic, and your needs and relationships will evolve. Regularly revisit your boundaries to ensure they still serve your personal growth and well-being. This ongoing process reflects a deep respect for yourself and your journey towards a more authentic and empowered life.

Incorporating boundary-setting into your life can significantly impact your personal development and the quality of your relationships. It empowers you to make choices that align with your values and needs, leading to a more fulfilling and authentic existence. As you become more adept at setting and maintaining boundaries, you'll find that your relationships become more meaningful, your self-respect deepens, and your personal growth accelerates. Remember, setting boundaries is not about creating distance but about nurturing healthy, respectful, and enriching connections with yourself and others.

Exercise n.20: Boundary Worksheet Exercise

Objective: Identify personal boundaries and practice setting them.
Type: Boundary-Setting Exercise
Duration: Weekly, for at least 15-20 minutes.

Instructions:
Set Aside Time: Dedicate 15-20 minutes each week for this exercise. Try to do it at the same time each week (e.g., Sunday evening).

Find a Quiet Space: Choose a calm and comfortable place where you won't be disturbed.

Weekly Reflection Prompts: Answer the following prompts each week:
- Identify Personal Boundaries: Reflect and write down where in your life you need to set boundaries. Consider aspects such as time, energy, personal space, emotional well-being, and relationships.
- Understand the Importance: For each boundary, write down why it is important to you and how it will protect your well-being.
- Plan for Communication: Identify who you need to set these boundaries with, and plan how you will communicate your boundaries clearly.
- Anticipate Challenges: Reflect on potential challenges you might face when setting these boundaries and how you will handle them.
- Practice Self-Compassion: Remind yourself that setting boundaries is an act of self-care. Write a compassionate statement to yourself, acknowledging that it's okay to prioritize your needs.

Document Your Reflections: Write down your weekly reflections. This will help you track your progress over time and reinforce your commitment to setting boundaries.

Consistency: Make this boundary worksheet exercise a non-negotiable part of your weekly routine to foster healthy boundaries and improve your well-being.

Gratitude and Positive Thinking

G ratitude and positive thinking are not just feel-good buzzwords but foundational elements that can transform your life from the inside out. When you begin to integrate gratitude into your daily routine, you start to shift your focus from what's lacking to appreciating what you already have. This subtle yet powerful change in perspective can dramatically alter how you interact with the world around you. Gratitude begets more gratitude, creating a cycle of positivity that can uplift your spirits even on the toughest days. It's about recognizing the good in your life and acknowledging that even in hardship, there are lessons and blessings to be found.

Positive thinking, on the other hand, is not about ignoring life's challenges but choosing to approach difficulties with a hopeful and optimistic mindset. It involves acknowledging the reality of a situation while believing in your ability to overcome it. This mindset doesn't just happen overnight; it's cultivated through consistent practice and a conscious decision to focus on the positive aspects of your life and the potential for good in every situation.

One practical way to start harnessing the power of gratitude and positive thinking is by keeping a gratitude journal. Each day, write down three things you're grateful for. These don't have to be monumental; even the simplest pleasures or achievements deserve recognition. This practice encourages you to seek out and celebrate the positive, no matter how small, which can significantly boost your mood and outlook on life.

Additionally, incorporating positive affirmations into your daily routine can reinforce your commitment to a positive mindset. Affirmations are positive statements that can help you to challenge and overcome self-sabotaging and negative thoughts. When you repeat them often, and believe in them, you can start to make positive changes in your life. For example, starting your day by affirming, "I am capable of overcoming any challenges that come my way," can set a positive tone for the day, empowering you to face whatever lies ahead with confidence and resilience.

Both gratitude and positive thinking are not passive activities but active exercises that require mindfulness and intentionality. They are about making a conscious choice every day to focus on the positive, to appreciate the present, and to maintain an optimistic outlook towards the future. This shift in mindset is not just beneficial for your mental and emotional health but can also have tangible effects on your physical well-being. Studies have shown that positive thinking and gratitude can improve your sleep, increase your lifespan, and even bolster your immune system.

As you embark on this journey of cultivating gratitude and positive thinking, remember that it's okay to have moments of negativity or doubt. The goal is not to achieve perfection but progress. With each step you take towards embracing gratitude and positivity, you are building a stronger, more resilient foundation for a fulfilling and joyful life.

Embracing gratitude and positive thinking extends beyond personal benefits; it also enhances your interactions and relationships with others. When you approach relationships with a grateful heart and a positive outlook, you naturally foster deeper connections and a more supportive network. This positive energy is contagious, encouraging a reciprocal flow of gratitude and kindness among your circle. By expressing appreciation for the people in your life, you not only strengthen your bonds but also create an environment where positivity thrives.

Moreover, the practice of gratitude and positive thinking empowers you to handle life's adversities with grace and resilience. Instead of being overwhelmed by stress or negativity, you learn to find the silver lining in every situation. This doesn't mean dismissing the complexity of your emotions but rather acknowledging them and focusing on what you can control - your attitude and response. By doing so, you cultivate a sense of peace and contentment, regardless of external circumstances.

To further integrate gratitude and positive thinking into your life, consider sharing your gratitude with others. Whether it's a simple thank you note, a heartfelt compliment, or acknowledging someone's impact on your life, these acts of kindness can significantly brighten someone's day and reinforce your own feelings of gratitude. Additionally, surrounding yourself with positive influences - people who uplift and encourage you - can help maintain your focus on the positive. Seek out communities, whether in-person or online, that support your journey towards a more grateful and optimistic mindset.

Remember, the practice of gratitude and positive thinking is a journey, not a destination. It's about making small, intentional choices each day that collectively lead to a more joyful and fulfilled life. Celebrate your progress, no matter how small, and be patient with yourself as you navigate this path. Over time, you'll find that these practices not only transform your outlook but also enrich your life in ways you never imagined possible.

Incorporating gratitude and positive thinking into your daily life is a powerful strategy for personal growth and happiness. By focusing on the good, practicing mindfulness, and expressing appreciation, you forge a path towards a more positive and resilient self. This approach not only benefits you but also has a profound impact on those around you, creating a cycle of positivity that can inspire and uplift everyone it touches.

Cultivating a Grateful Mindset

Gratitude is a transformative force that can reshape our perceptions, enhance our relationships, and improve our overall well-being. To cultivate a grateful mindset, it's essential to practice gratitude in both easy and challenging times. This means actively looking for things to be grateful for throughout your day, regardless of the circumstances. Start by acknowledging the simple joys and conveniences in your life, such as a warm cup of coffee in the morning or the comfort of your home. These acknowledgments, though small, lay the foundation for a deeper appreciation of life's blessings.

Implementing a gratitude practice into your daily routine can significantly amplify its benefits. Consider setting aside a few minutes each day to reflect on what you're thankful for. This could be in the morning, as you set the tone for your day, or in the evening, as you reflect on the day's events. Writing down these reflections in a journal can further solidify your gratitude practice, making it more tangible and meaningful.

Expanding your gratitude practice beyond personal reflection is also powerful. Expressing gratitude to others not only strengthens your relationships but also reinforces your own feelings of thankfulness. Take the time to verbally express appreciation to your loved ones, colleagues, and even strangers. A simple "thank you" can go a long way in making someone's day better and boosting your own mood.

Challenges and setbacks are inevitable, but they also present opportunities for gratitude. When faced with difficulties, try to find the lesson or silver lining in the situation. This doesn't mean dismissing your feelings but rather acknowledging them and then shifting your focus towards what can be learned or gained. This approach can transform obstacles into opportunities for growth and gratitude.

Mindfulness and gratitude are closely linked. By practicing mindfulness, you become more present and aware of the moment, which naturally enhances your ability to notice and appreciate the positive aspects of your life. Simple mindfulness exercises, such as deep breathing or mindful walking, can help you cultivate a state of awareness conducive to gratitude.

Celebrating the success of others is another facet of a grateful mindset. Instead of succumbing to envy or comparison, choose to be genuinely happy for the achievements and good fortune of others. This practice not only fosters a sense of community and connection but also amplifies your own capacity for joy and gratitude.

Gratitude in times of loss or grief can be particularly challenging, yet it remains a powerful tool for healing. Reflecting on the positive memories and the love shared with someone we've lost can be a comforting way to honor their impact on our lives. This form of gratitude acknowledges the pain of loss while also cherishing the beauty of the connection.

Nature and gratitude share a special relationship. Spending time in nature, observing its beauty and vastness, can elicit feelings of gratitude and humility. Whether it's a walk in the park, watching a sunset, or simply observing the intricate details of a flower, nature continually offers reasons to be grateful.

To truly **embed gratitude into your life**, it's important to make it a consistent practice rather than a sporadic effort. Like any habit, the more you practice gratitude, the more naturally it will come to you. Over time, this practice can shift your mindset, leading to a more joyful, fulfilled, and resilient life.

Gratitude as a shared practice can amplify its impact. Consider starting a gratitude circle with friends or family, where you share what you're grateful for on a regular basis. This not only strengthens your practice but also builds a supportive community focused on positivity and appreciation.

Lastly, remember that gratitude is a journey, not a destination. There will be days when feeling grateful comes easily, and others when it feels nearly impossible. The key is to keep returning to your practice, knowing that each act of gratitude is a step towards a more positive and empowered life.

The Science of Gratitude and Happiness

Delving into the **science of gratitude and happiness** reveals a fascinating intersection between psychology and neuroscience, illuminating how these practices can significantly impact our mental and emotional well-being. Research in the field of positive psychology has consistently shown that gratitude not only elevates our mood but also contributes to a myriad of health benefits, including reduced stress levels, improved heart health, and enhanced sleep quality. This body of evidence underscores the transformative power of gratitude, positioning it as a key component in the pursuit of happiness and a fulfilling life.

One pivotal study in this domain conducted by Robert A. Emmons and Michael E. McCullough found that individuals who kept weekly gratitude journals reported fewer physical symptoms, felt more optimistic about their lives, and experienced a greater sense of connection with others compared to those who did not engage in a gratitude practice. This study, among others, highlights how gratitude can reshape our perception of the world, helping us to focus on abundance rather than scarcity, which positively impacts our mental, emotional, and even physical health.

In addition to Emmons and McCullough's findings, neuroscientists have discovered that practicing gratitude can stimulate the brain's reward center, releasing dopamine and serotonin—chemicals that enhance mood and promote feelings of well-being. By activating these areas in the brain, gratitude works much like a natural antidepressant, lifting our spirits and fostering resilience. This physiological impact provides a scientific foundation for the idea that gratitude can rewire our brains, making us more inclined toward positivity over time.

Moreover, gratitude has been shown to reduce stress hormones like cortisol. When we engage in regular gratitude practices, we signal to our nervous system that we are in a safe, supportive environment, which helps calm the body and mind. This effect can be particularly beneficial during challenging times, giving us a psychological buffer that allows us to manage stress more effectively and bounce back from adversity with greater ease.

As research continues to reveal, gratitude isn't just a fleeting feeling—it's a mindset that promotes long-term happiness and well-being. By incorporating gratitude into our daily lives, we're not only enhancing our own health and resilience but also contributing to a more compassionate, connected world. As we close this chapter, remember that gratitude is a powerful tool that, when practiced consistently, can transform your life. It starts with small steps—a thank you, a moment of appreciation, a written reflection—and builds into a lasting, positive shift in your perspective.

Ultimately, gratitude allows us to see our lives through a lens of abundance and possibility. As you embrace this practice, you'll find yourself growing more resilient, more joyful, and better equipped to handle life's ups and downs with grace.

Exercise n.21: Gratitude Journal Exercise

Objective: Build a gratitude habit by journaling three things to be grateful for each evening.
Type: Daily Reflection Exercise
Duration: Daily, for at least 10-15 minutes.

Instructions:

Set Aside Time: Dedicate 10-15 minutes each evening for this exercise. Consistency is key, so try to do it at the same time each night (e.g., before bed).

Find a Quiet Space: Choose a calm and comfortable place where you won't be disturbed.

Daily Reflection Prompts: Answer the following prompts each evening:

- Reflect on Your Day: Take a few moments to reflect on the events of your day. Consider both the small and significant moments.
- Identify Three Things to Be Grateful For: Write down three specific things you are grateful for. These can be people, experiences, achievements, or simple pleasures.
- Describe Why You Are Grateful:
- For each item, write a brief description of why you are grateful for it and how it positively impacted your day.

Document Your Reflections: Use a notebook, a digital document, or a journaling app to record your daily reflections. This will help you track your gratitude over time and reinforce the habit.

Consistency: Make this gratitude journal exercise a non-negotiable part of your daily routine to foster a positive mindset and enhance your overall well-being.

Reframing Negative Thoughts

Reframing negative thoughts is a crucial skill that empowers you to shift your perspective, turning potentially debilitating thoughts into opportunities for growth and positivity. This process involves recognizing when you fall into negative thinking patterns and consciously choosing to interpret the situation differently. It's about finding a more positive or realistic spin on your thoughts and experiences. To begin, it's essential to identify the common negative thought patterns you might be experiencing. These can include all-or-nothing thinking, overgeneralization, focusing on the negatives while ignoring the positives, and catastrophizing, among others.

Once you've pinpointed these patterns, challenge them. Ask yourself whether these thoughts are truly accurate or if there's another way to view the situation. For instance, if you're thinking, "I'll never be good at this," consider whether there have been times when you've improved at a task with practice. This evidence contradicts the absolute of "never" and opens the door to a more balanced thought, such as, "I may not be skilled at this now, but I can improve with time and effort."

Another practical step is to practice gratitude. When negative thoughts arise, counterbalance them by thinking of three things you're grateful for. This practice can shift your focus from what's going wrong to what's going right, fostering a more positive outlook.

Mindfulness is also a powerful tool in reframing negative thoughts. It involves staying present and fully engaging with the current moment without judgment.

By observing your thoughts without getting caught up in them, you can gain distance and perspective, making it easier to challenge and reframe them.

Creating positive affirmations can further aid in this process. These are positive, empowering statements that counteract negative thoughts and build self-confidence. For example, transforming the thought, "I am not capable," into, "I am capable and strong," can significantly alter your mindset and approach to challenges.

Lastly, seek evidence that contradicts your negative thoughts. This can involve reflecting on past successes, considering the times when feared outcomes did not occur, or recognizing the support and resources you have available. This evidence can dismantle the foundation of your negative thoughts, making room for more positive and realistic perspectives.

Remember, reframing negative thoughts is a skill that requires practice. Be patient with yourself as you learn to navigate this process. With time and consistent effort, you can significantly alter your thought patterns, leading to improved mental well-being and a more positive outlook on life. Engaging in this practice not only benefits you but also positively impacts those around you, as your improved mood and outlook can influence your interactions and relationships in meaningful ways.

Recognizing Negative Thought Patterns

Recognizing negative thought patterns is a crucial step towards cultivating a mindset grounded in gratitude and positive thinking. These patterns, often deeply ingrained in our psyche, can significantly hinder our ability to see the abundance in our lives and to maintain an optimistic outlook. Negative thought patterns manifest in various forms, such as self-doubt, pessimism, and catastrophic thinking, where one tends to expect the worst possible outcome in any situation. The first step in addressing these harmful patterns is to become acutely aware of them. This awareness allows you to observe your thoughts without attaching to them emotionally, providing a clearer perspective on how these patterns influence your feelings and behaviors.

One effective strategy for recognizing these patterns is to maintain a **thought diary**. This simple yet powerful tool involves jotting down negative thoughts as they arise throughout the day. The act of writing helps to externalize these thoughts, making it easier to see them for what they truly are: mere thoughts, not facts. Over time, patterns will emerge, revealing the specific circumstances or triggers that tend to spark negative thinking. This insight is invaluable, as it enables you to anticipate and prepare for these triggers, gradually reducing their impact on your mindset.

Another approach is to challenge these negative thoughts directly. When you catch yourself slipping into a pattern of negative thinking, pause and ask yourself a series of questions designed to test the validity of these thoughts. For example, ask yourself, "Is there evidence to support this thought?" or "Is there a more positive and realistic way to view this situation?" This technique, known as **cognitive restructuring**, helps to break down irrational beliefs and replace them with more balanced and constructive thoughts.

Additionally, practicing **mindfulness** can be a powerful ally in recognizing and managing negative thought patterns. Mindfulness encourages you to live in the present moment and to observe your thoughts and feelings without judgment. By cultivating a regular mindfulness practice, you can develop the ability to detach from negative thoughts, viewing them as transient mental events rather than reflections of reality.

It's also beneficial to surround yourself with positive influences, whether they be uplifting books, podcasts, or individuals who embody the optimistic and grateful mindset you aspire to. These influences can serve as reminders of the power of positive thinking and the potential for personal growth and happiness.

Ultimately, the journey to overcoming negative thought patterns is ongoing and requires patience and persistence. It's about making a series of small, intentional changes that, over time, can lead to a profound transformation in how you view yourself and the world around you. By recognizing and addressing these patterns, you open the door to a life characterized by gratitude, resilience, and a deep-seated sense of fulfillment.

Thought Reframing Techniques

To effectively engage in **thought reframing**, it's essential to first acknowledge the power our internal dialogue holds over our emotions and behaviors. This technique involves consciously shifting our perspective on events, situations, or thoughts that may initially appear negative or distressing, transforming them into opportunities for growth, learning, or gratitude. One practical method to begin this process is the **ABCDE model**, a strategy rooted in cognitive-behavioral therapy that guides individuals through a series of steps to challenge and change their thought patterns.

A stands for **Antecedent**, which is the situation or event that triggers the negative thought. It's critical to pinpoint exactly what sparked the negative thinking. Was it a comment from a colleague, a personal mistake, or perhaps an unexpected event? Identifying the antecedent lays the groundwork for understanding and altering how you respond to similar situations in the future.

B represents **Beliefs**. These are the thoughts or assumptions you have about the event. Often, these beliefs are automatic and may not accurately reflect reality. They could be laden with distortions, such as overgeneralization or catastrophic thinking. By bringing these beliefs into the light, you can begin to question their validity.

C is for **Consequences**, which are the emotional and behavioral outcomes that result from your beliefs. This step involves recognizing how your beliefs about the antecedent affect how you feel and act. Do they lead to feelings of inadequacy, anxiety, or anger? Do they cause you to withdraw from others or give up on goals prematurely?

D stands for **Dispute**. This is the stage where you challenge your initial beliefs. Ask yourself, "Is there evidence that contradicts my belief? Could there be another way to view this situation? What would I tell a friend who had this thought?" This step is crucial for breaking down irrational or harmful beliefs and replacing them with more balanced and constructive ones.

E is for **Effective new belief**. This final step involves formulating a new, more rational, and positive belief to replace the old one. This new belief should acknowledge the reality of the situation without magnifying its negativity or impact. It should empower you to feel more in control and capable of handling similar situations differently in the future.

Incorporating this model into your daily routine can significantly impact how you perceive and react to challenges. It promotes a more flexible and resilient mindset, allowing you to navigate life's ups and downs with greater ease and confidence. Moreover, by practicing thought reframing regularly, you cultivate a more positive and grateful outlook on life, one that recognizes challenges as opportunities for growth and values the lessons learned from every experience.

Additionally, **positive visualization** can complement thought reframing by helping you imagine the successful application of your new beliefs in future scenarios. This technique not only reinforces your new, constructive beliefs but also prepares you mentally to act in ways that are consistent with these beliefs, thereby fostering a cycle of positive thinking and behavior.

Engaging in thought reframing is not about denying the reality of difficult situations or emotions. Instead, it's about choosing to focus on aspects within your control, such as your reactions and mindset. By doing so, you empower yourself to lead a life marked by resilience, gratitude, and positivity. This approach does not promise a life free from challenges, but it does offer the tools to face them with strength and optimism, ensuring that you remain anchored in your values and committed to your personal growth, regardless of the circumstances.

Exercise n.22: Thought Reframing Practice Exercise

Objective: Practice reframing negative thoughts into positive or constructive ones to improve mindset.
Type: Mindset Exercise
Duration: Daily, for at least 10-15 minutes.

Instructions:
Set Aside Time: Dedicate 10-15 minutes each day for this exercise. Consistency is key, so try to do it at the same time each day (e.g., in the evening).

Find a Quiet Space: Choose a calm and comfortable place where you won't be disturbed.

Daily Reflection Prompts: Answer the following prompts each day:

- Identify Negative Thoughts: Reflect on your day and write down any negative thoughts you experienced. Be specific about what the thoughts were and when they occurred.
- Understand the Impact: Reflect on how these negative thoughts made you feel and how they impacted your behavior or mood.
- Reframe the Thoughts: Challenge each negative thought by considering alternative and more positive perspectives. Write down a reframed version of each negative thought.
- Reflect on the Reframing: how the reframed thoughts make you feel? How could they positively impact your behavior or mood?

Document Your Reflections: Use a notebook, a digital document, or a journaling app to record your daily reflections. This will help you track your progress over time and reinforce the habit of positive thinking.

Consistency: Make this thought reframing practice a non-negotiable part of your daily routine to foster a positive mindset and improve overall well-being.

Building Positivity Daily

Incorporating positivity into your daily life is not just about adopting an optimistic mindset; it's about creating a lifestyle that fosters positive thinking through every action and reaction. **Positive affirmations** can be a transformative tool in this process. Start your day by affirming your worth, strengths, and capabilities. Phrases like "I am capable of overcoming any challenge that comes my way" or "Today, I choose joy and gratitude over fear and doubt" can set a powerful tone for the day.

Gratitude practices extend beyond the gratitude journal. Engage in small acts of gratitude throughout your day. This could be as simple as mentally acknowledging something you're grateful for every time you take a sip of water or sending a quick text to someone expressing appreciation for their presence in your life. These moments of gratitude can significantly elevate your mood and outlook.

Mindful consumption plays a crucial role in building positivity. Be intentional about the media you consume, the conversations you partake in, and the thoughts you entertain. Replace negative news or gossip with uplifting podcasts, books, or articles. Engage in conversations that leave you feeling inspired and energized rather than drained or pessimistic.

Physical activity is another pillar of a positive lifestyle. Exercise releases endorphins, often referred to as happiness hormones, which can improve mood and reduce feelings of anxiety and depression. Find an activity you enjoy, whether it's yoga, running, dancing, or hiking, and make it a regular part of your routine.

Social connections are vital. Surround yourself with people who uplift you and share your values of positivity and growth. These relationships can provide support, laughter, and a sense of belonging, all of which are essential for maintaining a positive outlook on life.

Learning and growth opportunities should be embraced as they come. Adopting a mindset that views challenges as opportunities for growth rather than insurmountable obstacles can significantly impact your overall positivity. When faced with a difficult situation, ask yourself, "What can I learn from this?" or "How can this experience help me grow?"

Self-care is non-negotiable. It's difficult to maintain a positive outlook if you're running on empty. Ensure you're getting enough sleep, eating nourishing foods, and giving yourself permission to relax and enjoy hobbies or activities that bring you joy.

Random acts of kindness can not only boost the recipient's mood but can significantly enhance your own sense of well-being and positivity. The act of giving, without expecting anything in return, can foster a deep sense of fulfillment and happiness.

By integrating these practices into your daily life, you create a fertile ground for positivity to grow and flourish. It's about making conscious choices every day to focus on the good, practice gratitude, and engage in activities that nurture your mind, body, and spirit. This approach to life doesn't mean ignoring the challenges or difficulties you may face but choosing to respond to them with resilience, optimism, and a belief in your ability to navigate through them. Remember, building positivity is a journey that involves small, intentional steps each day towards a more joyful, grateful, and fulfilling life.

Positive Affirmations & Visualization

Harnessing the power of **positive affirmations** and **visualization** requires a deliberate and thoughtful approach, one that integrates these practices seamlessly into your daily life. Positive affirmations are short, powerful statements that, when spoken with conviction, can shift your mindset, influence your subconscious mind, and manifest changes in your life. Visualization, on the other hand, is the process of creating vivid, detailed mental images of the outcomes you desire, engaging all your senses to make these imagined scenarios feel as real as possible. Together, these techniques can significantly amplify your ability to foster positivity and resilience, guiding you towards a life of fulfillment and joy.

To effectively incorporate positive affirmations into your routine, start by identifying areas in your life where you seek improvement or face challenges. Perhaps you wish to cultivate more self-confidence, enhance your productivity, or foster deeper connections in your relationships. Once you have pinpointed these areas, craft affirmations that resonate deeply with you and reflect the positive outcomes you aspire to achieve. For example, if you aim to boost your self-confidence, an affirmation like "I am confident in my abilities and make valuable contributions to the world" can be incredibly empowering. Repeat these affirmations daily, ideally in the morning as you start your day or during moments of self-reflection. The key is to recite them with feeling and conviction, allowing the words to penetrate your thoughts and influence your actions.

Visualization complements the practice of affirmations by providing a rich, sensory experience that further embeds these positive beliefs into your psyche. To visualize effectively, find a quiet space where you can relax without interruptions. Close your eyes and imagine achieving one of your desired outcomes, such as successfully completing a project at work or enjoying a harmonious relationship with a loved one. Picture the scene in as much detail as possible, focusing on the sights, sounds, and emotions associated with this success. Feel the joy, pride, or love as if it were happening in that very moment. By regularly engaging in this practice, you train your brain to recognize these positive outcomes as attainable, thereby motivating you to take the necessary steps to make them a reality.

Both affirmations and visualization are most impactful when practiced consistently and with intention. They are not quick fixes but rather powerful tools for shaping your mindset and, by extension, your life. As you integrate these practices into your daily routine, remember to be patient and kind to yourself. Change takes time, and setbacks are a natural part of the growth process. Celebrate your progress, no matter how small, and trust that with each affirmation and visualization, you are laying the groundwork for a life filled with positivity, resilience, and genuine happiness.

Moreover, it's beneficial to surround yourself with reminders of your affirmations and visualizations. Consider creating a vision board filled with images and words that represent your goals and aspirations. Place it somewhere you will see it daily to serve as a constant source of inspiration and motivation. Alternatively, set reminders on your phone to pause and recite your affirmations or take a few moments for visualization throughout the day. These small acts can make a profound difference in maintaining your focus and commitment to your personal growth journey.

Incorporating positive affirmations and visualization into your life is a transformative process that encourages a shift in perspective from what is lacking to what is abundantly possible. It fosters an attitude of gratitude and opens your heart and mind to the endless opportunities for growth, learning, and connection. By affirming your worth and visualizing your success, you not only enhance your own well-being but also become a beacon of positivity and strength for those around you. Engage in these practices with an open heart and a willing spirit, and watch as the world opens up in response to your positive energy and intent.

Practicing Joyful Daily Rituals

Joyful daily rituals are the cornerstone of cultivating a life filled with positivity and resilience. By establishing routines that nurture joy and gratitude, individuals can significantly enhance their emotional well-being and overall quality of life. These rituals don't have to be time-consuming or elaborate; rather, they should be simple practices that can be seamlessly integrated into everyday life, bringing a sense of peace, fulfillment, and happiness.

One effective ritual is starting the day with a moment of **gratitude**. Before even getting out of bed, take a few minutes to think of three things you're grateful for. This could be as simple as the comfort of your bed, the warmth of the sun, or the presence of loved ones in your life. This practice sets a positive tone for the day, shifting your focus from what you lack to what you have, fostering an attitude of abundance.

Another joyful ritual involves creating moments of **mindfulness** throughout the day. This could be a brief pause to take a deep breath and center yourself before a meeting or enjoying a cup of tea without distractions. These moments of mindfulness allow you to reconnect with the present, reducing stress and enhancing your capacity for joy and gratitude.

Creating a joy journal is another powerful ritual. Unlike a traditional journal, a joy journal focuses exclusively on positive experiences, moments of happiness, and reasons for gratitude. Each evening, write down at least one thing that brought you joy that day. Over time, this practice can shift your perspective, making you more attuned to the positive aspects of your life.

Engaging in acts of kindness is a ritual that not only brings joy to others but also to yourself. Whether it's a simple compliment, helping a neighbor, or volunteering, these acts of kindness generate a profound sense of happiness and connection with others. They remind us of the impact we can have on the world around us and the joy that comes from giving without expectation of return.

Incorporating **movement into your daily routine** is also vital. This doesn't necessarily mean rigorous exercise but rather any form of movement that you enjoy and that brings you happiness. It could be dancing to your favorite song, a short walk in nature, or a gentle yoga session. Movement releases endorphins, enhances mood, and is a powerful way to celebrate and appreciate your body.

Lastly, **savoring the simple pleasures** in life can be a transformative ritual. This means truly being present and finding joy in everyday experiences, whether it's savoring a delicious meal, enjoying the texture of soft fabric, or observing the beauty of nature. These moments of savoring deeply enrich our lives, reminding us of the beauty and abundance that surrounds us.

By integrating these joyful daily rituals into your life, you create a foundation of positivity and gratitude that can support you through challenges and enhance your overall well-being. These practices encourage a mindful appreciation of the present moment, deepen connections with others, and foster a resilient, joyful spirit. Remember, the goal is not to add more to your to-do list but to weave moments of joy and gratitude into the fabric of your daily life, making positivity a natural and effortless part of your existence.

Exercise n.23: Daily Positivity Ritual Exercise

Objective: Create a daily ritual focused on joy, gratitude, or positive affirmations to foster a positive mindset.
Type: Routine-Building Exercise
Duration: Daily, for at least 10-15 minutes.

Instructions:
Set Aside Time: Dedicate 10-15 minutes each day for this exercise. Consistency is key, so try to do it at the same time each day (e.g., in the morning or before bed).

Find a Quiet Space: Choose a calm and comfortable place where you won't be disturbed.

Choose Your Positivity Focus: Decide whether you want to focus on joy, gratitude, or positive affirmations for your daily ritual.

Daily Ritual Steps: Follow these steps each day based on your chosen focus:
- Joy: Reflect on moments of joy from your day or anticipate joyful activities. Write down or visualize these moments, allowing yourself to fully experience the positive emotions.
- Gratitude: Write down three things you are grateful for. Be specific and reflect on why you are grateful for each item. Allow yourself to feel the gratitude deeply.
- Positive Affirmations: Write down or recite three positive affirmations. These should be empowering statements that reinforce your self-belief and confidence. Repeat each affirmation several times with conviction.

Document Your Ritual: Use a notebook, a digital document, or a journaling app to record your daily ritual. This will help you track your progress over time and reinforce the habit.

Consistency: Make this daily positivity ritual a non-negotiable part of your routine to foster a positive mindset and enhance overall well-being.

Sustaining Growth and Transformation

To sustain growth and transformation, it is essential to recognize that personal development is a continuous process, not a destination. This understanding forms the bedrock of a mindset geared towards lifelong learning and adaptability. One fundamental aspect of this journey is setting **realistic goals**. These goals should stretch your capabilities but remain achievable. They serve as milestones on the path to growth, providing direction and a sense of purpose. However, it's crucial to approach goal-setting with flexibility, allowing for adjustments as you gain new insights and experiences.

Another key element is **feedback**. Seeking and constructively using feedback from trusted sources can illuminate areas for improvement that you might not see on your own. It's an invaluable tool for personal and professional development. Yet, it's equally important to cultivate self-compassion. Growth often involves stepping out of your comfort zone and facing challenges head-on, which can lead to setbacks. Viewing these setbacks as learning opportunities rather than failures fosters resilience and a positive attitude towards personal growth.

Reflective practices such as journaling or meditation offer another avenue for sustaining growth. They encourage introspection, helping you to stay aligned with your core values and purpose. This alignment ensures that your efforts towards growth are meaningful and fulfilling. Reflective practices also promote mental clarity, reducing stress and enhancing decision-making abilities.

Engaging in **lifelong learning** is another cornerstone of sustained growth. This can take many forms, from formal education to self-directed learning. The key is to remain curious and open to new ideas and perspectives. Lifelong learning not only expands your knowledge and skills but also keeps your mind sharp and adaptable.

Building a **support network** is equally critical. Surrounding yourself with people who inspire, challenge, and support you can significantly impact your growth journey. These relationships provide encouragement, advice, and a sense of belonging, all of which are vital for personal development.

Lastly, it's important to **celebrate progress**. Recognizing and appreciating your achievements, no matter how small, boosts motivation and self-esteem. It's a reminder of how far you've come and a reinforcement of your ability to achieve your goals. Celebrating progress also includes acknowledging the effort and dedication you've put into your growth, reinforcing the value of perseverance and hard work.

As you continue to navigate the path of personal growth, remember that transformation is a series of small steps. Each step, each decision, and each action contributes to the larger journey of becoming your best self. By embracing these principles, you lay a strong foundation for sustained growth and transformation, setting the stage for a fulfilling and empowered life.

Embracing the concept of **incremental progress** is crucial in the pursuit of sustained growth and transformation. This approach acknowledges that significant changes often result from small, consistent steps rather than monumental leaps. Incremental progress is about celebrating every bit of advancement and understanding that each action, no matter how minor it may seem, contributes to larger goals. This mindset helps to maintain motivation and persistence, even when the path forward appears daunting.

Adapting to change plays a pivotal role in sustaining growth. In a world that is constantly evolving, the ability to adapt is invaluable. This means being willing to reassess and adjust your goals and strategies in response to new information or circumstances. Adaptability ensures that you remain relevant and effective in your personal and professional life, enabling you to overcome obstacles and seize opportunities as they arise.

Practicing gratitude is another essential element. By focusing on what you are thankful for, you cultivate an attitude of abundance rather than scarcity. Gratitude shifts your focus from what is lacking to what is present, enriching your life with a deeper appreciation for the people, experiences, and opportunities that shape your journey. This perspective fosters resilience, happiness, and a greater sense of satisfaction.

Mindset management is key to enduring growth and transformation. Cultivating a growth mindset, where challenges are viewed as opportunities for learning and failure is seen as a stepping stone to success, is fundamental. This perspective encourages risk-taking, experimentation, and perseverance, all of which are critical for personal development. Mindset management involves being mindful of self-talk, challenging limiting beliefs, and embracing the belief that abilities and intelligence can be developed.

Physical well-being cannot be overlooked in the quest for sustained growth. Regular physical activity, adequate rest, and nutritious eating habits all play a significant role in maintaining the energy, focus, and stamina required for personal development. When you take care of your body, you create a strong foundation for mental and emotional well-being, enabling you to tackle challenges with vigor and resilience.

Digital detoxing and managing screen time is increasingly becoming a vital part of sustaining growth. In an age where digital distractions are omnipresent, setting boundaries around technology use can help preserve mental energy and foster deeper, more meaningful connections with others and with oneself. Periodic disconnection from digital devices allows for reflection, creativity, and engagement in activities that nourish the soul.

Environmental influences also significantly impact our ability to sustain growth. Creating a physical and social environment that supports your growth goals can enhance your progress. This might involve organizing your living and working spaces to reduce clutter and distraction, or it could mean choosing to spend time with individuals who inspire and uplift you. The environments in which we live and work can either propel us forward or hold us back, making it crucial to curate spaces that align with our growth aspirations.

Incorporating these principles into your life requires intentionality and commitment. However, the rewards of sustained growth and transformation are immeasurable. By adopting a holistic approach that encompasses mental, emotional, physical, and environmental well-being, you set the stage for a life characterized by continuous learning, resilience, and fulfillment. Each step forward, no matter how small, is a victory in the journey of personal evolution, leading to a richer, more meaningful existence.

Embracing Lifelong Growth

Embracing lifelong growth requires a commitment to **constant learning** and **adaptability**. This process involves recognizing that personal development is an ongoing journey, not a destination. To sustain growth and transformation, it's vital to cultivate a mindset that embraces change and sees potential growth opportunities in every experience. **Setting realistic and achievable goals** is a crucial step in this journey. These goals should be aligned with one's core values and purpose, serving as a compass guiding towards personal growth.

Reflecting on experiences and learning from both successes and failures are fundamental practices. Reflection allows for a deeper understanding of one's actions and decisions, fostering a growth mindset. It's also essential to seek feedback from others, as it provides different perspectives and insights that can lead to significant personal development.

Investing in oneself is another key aspect of embracing lifelong growth. This can take various forms, such as pursuing further education, learning new skills, or engaging in activities that challenge and stretch personal capabilities. Surrounding oneself with **like-minded individuals** who are also committed to personal growth can offer support, motivation, and accountability.

Practicing resilience in the face of challenges and setbacks is crucial. Developing coping strategies and maintaining a positive outlook can help navigate through difficult times, turning obstacles into opportunities for growth. **Emotional intelligence** plays a significant role in this aspect, as it involves understanding and managing one's emotions, as well as recognizing and influencing the emotions of others in a positive way.

Adopting healthy habits and routines supports physical, mental, and emotional well-being, all of which are foundational to personal growth. Regular exercise, a balanced diet, sufficient sleep, and mindfulness practices are examples of habits that can enhance one's capacity for sustained growth and transformation.

Finally, **embracing change** and staying open to new experiences encourage flexibility and adaptability. Being willing to step out of one's comfort zone and explore new horizons can lead to unexpected opportunities for growth and learning.

The Importance of a Growth Mindset

Cultivating a **growth mindset** is foundational to embracing lifelong growth, as it empowers individuals to view challenges not as insurmountable obstacles but as opportunities for development and learning. This perspective shift is crucial for anyone seeking to enhance their inner strength and resilience. A growth mindset fosters the belief that abilities and intelligence can be developed through dedication, hard work, and persistence. It's about understanding that every experience, whether perceived as positive or negative, contributes to learning and personal growth.

To develop a growth mindset, one must first become mindful of their internal dialogue. It's common to encounter self-imposed limits and doubts that can hinder progress. Recognizing these thoughts as merely thoughts, not truths, allows for the reprogramming of one's mindset. For instance, instead of thinking, "I'm not good at this," one could reframe this thought to, "What am I missing? How can I approach this differently to improve?" This subtle shift in thinking opens up a world of possibilities for personal development and problem-solving.

Embracing challenges is another pillar of a growth mindset. Instead of avoiding difficulties for fear of failure, see each challenge as a chance to stretch your abilities and grow. It's through tackling these challenges head-on that skills are honed, and confidence is built. When faced with setbacks, instead of labeling them as failures, view them as feedback. This feedback is invaluable for learning and adjusting strategies moving forward.

Continuous learning plays a significant role in maintaining a growth mindset. The pursuit of knowledge and new skills should be seen as a lifelong endeavor. This can mean reading extensively, taking courses, attending workshops, or simply being curious about the world around you. Every piece of new knowledge acquired is a step towards becoming a more well-rounded, resilient individual.

Furthermore, fostering **perseverance** is essential. The journey towards personal growth is rarely linear. There will be times of stagnation and moments of doubt. However, perseverance lies in the commitment to keep moving forward, even when progress seems slow. It's about recognizing that growth happens over time, and with each small step, you are getting closer to your goals.

Incorporating feedback constructively is also a key aspect of a growth mindset. Seeking out and being open to feedback can provide insights that one might not have considered. It's important to listen, reflect, and then act on this feedback without taking it as a personal critique. This approach can significantly accelerate personal growth and lead to improved outcomes.

Lastly, a growth mindset encourages the **celebration of successes**, no matter how small. Acknowledging and appreciating these wins boosts motivation and reinforces the belief in one's ability to grow and succeed. It's a reminder that effort and attitude are just as important as the outcome.

By adopting these practices, individuals can foster a growth mindset that will serve them well in all areas of life. It's about making a conscious choice to remain open, adaptable, and always in pursuit of growth. This mindset not only enhances personal development but also contributes to a more fulfilling and resilient life.

Adapting to Life's Changes

Life's unpredictability demands a resilience that is both cultivated and refined over time. This resilience is not innate; it is built through deliberate practice and the conscious choice to face challenges head-on. **Adapting to life's changes** requires a multifaceted approach, starting with the acknowledgment that change is the only constant. Acceptance of this fact is the first step towards building a resilient mindset. It involves letting go of the illusion of control over external circumstances and focusing instead on what can be controlled: your reactions, your mindset, and your actions.

Developing resilience is akin to strengthening a muscle; it grows more robust with use. Facing small adversities and navigating through them successfully builds confidence in one's ability to handle bigger challenges. This confidence is bolstered by **self-awareness**, understanding your emotional responses, and recognizing your triggers. It allows for a more measured and effective approach to problem-solving, ensuring that emotions do not cloud judgment.

Flexibility plays a crucial role in adapting to change. It involves the willingness to pivot and adjust strategies when faced with new information or when the original plan is no longer viable. This flexibility is not about aimless wandering but about intentional redirection, keeping your core values and goals in focus while navigating the changing landscapes of life.

Support systems cannot be underestimated in their importance. Surrounding yourself with a network of supportive relationships provides a safety net during times of change. These relationships offer emotional sustenance, practical advice, and sometimes, a much-needed external perspective. Cultivating a community of people who believe in your growth and resilience adds an invaluable layer of strength to your journey.

Learning from experience is another critical aspect of adapting with resilience. Every encounter with change, whether perceived as positive or negative, holds valuable lessons. Reflecting on these experiences to extract insights and applying these lessons to future challenges accelerates personal growth and fortifies resilience. It transforms experiences into stepping stones rather than stumbling blocks.

Moreover, maintaining a **proactive attitude** towards personal development ensures that you are better equipped to deal with whatever life throws your way. This means consistently seeking out opportunities for growth, whether through formal education, new hobbies, or challenging assignments at work. A proactive approach keeps you moving forward, even in the face of uncertainty.

Practicing **self-compassion** during times of change is essential. Being harsh or critical towards oneself only adds to the stress and makes the process of adaptation more difficult. Recognizing that setbacks are part of the growth process, and treating yourself with the same kindness and understanding that you would offer a friend, can significantly ease the transition.

Lastly, embracing a **lifestyle of mindfulness** can enhance resilience. Mindfulness practices such as meditation, deep breathing, and yoga can help maintain an equilibrium amidst chaos. These practices ground you in the present moment, making it easier to navigate the complexities of change with a calm and clear mind.

By integrating these strategies into your life, adapting to change becomes less about merely surviving and more about thriving. It's about viewing each change, each challenge, as an opportunity to learn, grow, and become a more resilient version of yourself. Resilience, then, becomes not just a tool for coping with life's changes but a pathway to a more empowered and intentional life.

Exercise n.24: Growth Mindset Journal Exercise

Objective: Reinforce a lifelong growth mindset by documenting moments of growth and learning.
Type: Reflection Exercise
Duration: Daily, for at least 10-15 minutes.

Instructions:
Set Aside Time: Dedicate 10-15 minutes each day for this exercise. Consistency is key, so try to do it at the same time each day (e.g., in the evening).

Find a Quiet Space: Choose a calm and comfortable place where you won't be disturbed.

Daily Reflection Prompts: Answer the following prompts each day:
*   Identify Moments of Growth: Reflect on your day and write down any moments where you experienced growth or learning. These can be big or small, personal or professional.
*   Describe the Experience: Describe the situation or activity that led to your growth. Be specific about what happened and how you responded.
*   Reflect on the Learning: Reflect on what you learned from the experience. Consider how this learning contributes to your personal or professional development.
*   Plan for Application: Identify how you can apply this new knowledge or skill in the future. Write down specific actions you can take to continue growing in this area.

Document Your Reflections: Use a notebook, a digital document, or a journaling app to record your daily reflections. This will help you track your progress over time and reinforce the habit of a growth mindset.

Consistency: Make this growth mindset journal exercise a non-negotiable part of your daily routine to foster continuous learning and personal development.

Personal Empowerment Plan

To create a **Personal Empowerment Plan**, begin by setting clear, actionable goals that reflect your core values and desired areas of growth. These goals should be specific, measurable, attainable, relevant, and time-bound (SMART). For each goal, outline the steps necessary to achieve it, breaking down larger objectives into smaller, manageable tasks. This approach not only simplifies the process but also makes progress easier to track and celebrate.

Identify the resources and tools you'll need to support your journey. These might include books, courses, apps, or even mentors and support groups. Having a toolkit at your disposal ensures you're prepared to tackle challenges and seize opportunities for learning and development.

Establish a routine for regular self-reflection and adjustment. Set aside time weekly or monthly to review your progress, reflect on what you've learned, and make any necessary adjustments to your plan. This iterative process allows you to stay aligned with your goals and adapt to any changes in your circumstances or priorities.

Incorporate practices that nurture your mental, emotional, and physical well-being. Activities such as meditation, exercise, and journaling can enhance your resilience, focus, and overall health, providing a strong foundation for personal growth.

Build accountability into your plan. Share your goals with a trusted friend, family member, or mentor who can offer support, encouragement, and constructive feedback. Accountability partners not only motivate you but also help you stay committed to your path, even when faced with obstacles.

Celebrate your achievements, no matter how small. Recognizing and rewarding yourself for the progress you make fosters a positive mindset and motivates you to continue striving towards your goals.

Finally, remain flexible and open to change. Your Personal Empowerment Plan is a living document that should evolve as you grow and learn. Be willing to revise your goals and strategies as needed to reflect your changing aspirations and insights gained along the way.

By following these steps, you can develop a comprehensive and adaptable Personal Empowerment Plan that guides you towards sustained growth and transformation. This plan serves as a roadmap, helping you navigate the complexities of personal development with clarity, purpose, and resilience.

Setting Goals for Improvement

When embarking on the path of ongoing improvement, setting goals becomes an indispensable practice, one that requires careful thought and strategic planning. To ensure that these goals are not just mere aspirations but achievable milestones, they should be deeply rooted in your personal values and the broader vision you have for your life. This alignment guarantees that every goal you set is a step forward in your journey of personal empowerment and growth.

The first step in this process involves a deep dive into understanding what truly matters to you. This understanding forms the bedrock of your goals, ensuring they resonate with your innermost desires and ambitions. From this place of clarity, begin to map out your goals, giving each a defined shape with specific criteria that measure success. This specificity transforms vague wishes into tangible targets.

As you chart these goals, it's crucial to infuse each with a sense of realism. While it's important to stretch and challenge yourself, setting goals far beyond your reach can lead to frustration and demotivation. Find that sweet spot where a goal is ambitious enough to motivate you but realistic enough to be attainable with dedicated effort. This balance is key to maintaining enthusiasm and momentum in your growth journey.

In addition to setting individual goals, consider the broader timeline and how these goals fit into your life's tapestry. Some goals may be short-term, acting as stepping stones to larger aspirations, while others may be long-term, requiring sustained effort and commitment. Organizing your goals along a timeline helps in prioritizing actions and allocating resources effectively, ensuring that you're not just busy, but productive in your pursuit of growth.

Another vital aspect of goal setting for ongoing improvement is the establishment of milestones. These are markers of progress, small victories along the way that keep you motivated and engaged. Celebrating these milestones is crucial; it reinforces the positive behavior and effort that got you there and fuels your drive to continue pushing forward.

To keep your goals aligned with your evolving self, periodic reviews are essential. Life is dynamic, and so are you. What seemed important at one point may lose its relevance, or you might discover new interests and areas for growth. Regularly revisiting and, if necessary, revising your goals ensures that your path of improvement remains aligned with who you are becoming, not just who you were when you set those goals.

Incorporating feedback into this process, both from your own reflections and from trusted others, can provide invaluable insights that refine your goals further. This feedback loop, a continuous process of action, reflection, learning, and adjustment, is the cornerstone of a growth mindset and ongoing improvement.

As you work towards these goals, remember to be kind to yourself. Progress is rarely linear, and setbacks are part of the process. Each setback is an opportunity to learn, to reassess, and to come back stronger. Maintaining a positive, resilient attitude in the face of challenges is itself a goal worth pursuing, one that will serve you well across all areas of life.

Finally, while the focus here is on setting goals for ongoing improvement, the underlying thread is the journey towards becoming the best version of yourself. Each goal, each step forward, is a piece of the puzzle, contributing to the larger picture of your life. By approaching this process with intention, dedication, and a willingness to learn and adapt, you set the stage for a life of growth, fulfillment, and ever-deepening self-awareness.

Monthly Self-Reflection and Adjustment

The practice of monthly self-reflection and adjustment is a cornerstone of personal growth, allowing individuals to pause, evaluate their progress, and recalibrate their actions according to the insights gained. This disciplined approach ensures that your Personal Empowerment Plan remains a dynamic tool, finely tuned to your evolving needs, goals, and circumstances. It is here, in this space of quiet contemplation and honest assessment, that you can most effectively measure the distance traveled and plot the course ahead with renewed focus and clarity.

Begin each monthly reflection session by revisiting your goals, both the short-term objectives set for the month and the long-term aspirations that frame your overall journey. Assess your achievements with an open heart, acknowledging the efforts made and the progress achieved, no matter how incremental. It's important to approach this evaluation without judgment, viewing each experience as valuable feedback rather than a measure of success or failure. This mindset fosters a culture of continuous learning and improvement, where every outcome serves as a stepping stone towards greater understanding and mastery.

Equally critical is the assessment of challenges encountered along the way. Reflect on the obstacles that impeded your progress, identifying their sources and considering the strategies employed to address them. This analysis is not about assigning blame but about uncovering patterns, recognizing areas of resistance, and understanding the underlying factors that influence your behavior and decisions. By dissecting these challenges, you gain actionable insights that can inform your approach moving forward, turning potential setbacks into powerful catalysts for growth and change.

In this reflective process, also consider the habits and routines that shape your daily life. Evaluate their alignment with your goals and core values, discerning which practices serve your highest good and which may be hindering your progress. This scrutiny allows you to make conscious choices about where to invest your energy, ensuring that your actions are intentional, and your lifestyle is conducive to the realization of your aspirations.

Adjustment, the natural counterpart to reflection, involves taking the insights gained and translating them into actionable steps. This may mean setting new goals, modifying existing ones, or changing tactics altogether. The key is to remain flexible and responsive to the feedback received, allowing your plan to evolve in harmony with your personal growth journey. Adjustments might also involve seeking out additional resources, whether in the form of knowledge, skills, or support networks, to overcome obstacles and capitalize on opportunities for advancement.

As you make these adjustments, it's crucial to maintain a forward-looking perspective, focusing on the possibilities that lie ahead rather than dwelling on past difficulties. Envision the path forward with optimism and determination, setting realistic and inspiring goals for the coming month. This proactive stance not only propels you towards your long-term vision but also cultivates a sense of agency and empowerment, reinforcing your ability to shape your own destiny.

Finally, the practice of monthly self-reflection and adjustment is an act of self-care, a commitment to nurturing your growth and well-being with intention and compassion. It's a time to celebrate your resilience, honor your journey, and recommit to your personal empowerment plan with a renewed sense of purpose and passion. By embracing this practice, you ensure that your path towards growth and transformation is not only sustained but also enriched with deeper understanding, adaptability, and a steadfast commitment to realizing your fullest potential.

Exercise n.25: Monthly Self-Assessment Exercise

Objective: Track personal growth and adjust goals monthly.
Type: Self-Reflection Exercise
Duration: Monthly, for at least 30-45 minutes.

Instructions:
Set Aside Time: Dedicate 30-45 minutes at the end of each month for this exercise. Consistency is key, so try to do it at the same time each month (e.g., the last Sunday of the month).

Find a Quiet Space: Choose a calm and comfortable place.

Monthly Reflection Prompts: Answer these prompts monthly:

- Review Goals: Reflect on the goals you set for the month. Write down each goal and note whether you achieved it or not. If not, consider what obstacles you encountered.
- Celebrate Achievements: Identify and celebrate any achievements, no matter how small. Reflect on what went well and why.
- Assess Challenges: Reflect on any challenges or setbacks you faced. Consider what you learned from these experiences and how you can overcome similar obstacles in the future.
- Identify Areas for Growth: Reflect on areas where you want to continue growing. Write down specific skills, habits, or behaviors you want to develop.
- Set New Goals: Based on your reflections, set new goals for the upcoming month. Ensure they are SMART (Specific, Measurable, Achievable, Relevant, Time-bound).
- Plan Actions: Outline specific actions you will take to achieve your new goals. Identify any resources or support you might need.

Document Your Reflections: Record monthly reflections in a notebook, digital document, or journaling app to track progress and reinforce self-assessment.

Consistency: Make monthly self-assessments a mandatory routine for continuous growth and goal adjustment.

Finding Support and Accountability

To foster an environment of support and accountability, it's crucial to actively seek and build a network that aligns with your goals for personal growth and transformation. **Finding like-minded individuals** who share similar aspirations can significantly enhance your journey, providing both motivation and a sense of community. This can be achieved through various means, such as joining local or online groups focused on self-improvement, mindfulness, or any other area of interest that contributes to your growth. Engaging in these communities not only offers you the chance to receive support but also to give back, creating a reciprocal relationship of growth and learning.

Accountability partnerships are another powerful tool in sustaining growth. Pairing up with someone who is also committed to personal development can make the process more manageable and enjoyable. These partnerships allow for regular check-ins, where both parties can share successes, challenges, and insights, fostering a space where honesty and encouragement thrive. When selecting an accountability partner, it's important to choose someone who is reliable, supportive, and willing to provide constructive feedback when necessary.

Setting up regular meetings with your accountability partner or support group is essential. These meetings can be in person or virtual, depending on what works best for everyone involved. During these sessions, discuss what you've been working on, the obstacles you've encountered, and the progress you've made. This not only keeps you accountable but also encourages you to reflect on your journey and strategize for the future.

Leveraging technology can also play a significant role in finding support and maintaining accountability. Numerous apps and platforms are designed to track progress, set reminders for habits and goals, and connect with others on similar paths. Utilizing these tools can help keep you on track and in touch with your support network, ensuring that you're never alone in your journey.

Being open to feedback is another critical aspect of building a supportive and accountable environment. Feedback from others can provide valuable perspectives that you may not have considered, offering opportunities for growth and improvement. Approach feedback with an open mind and a willingness to learn, and remember to express gratitude to those who take the time to offer their insights.

Celebrating milestones together with your support network reinforces the positive impact of your collective efforts. Acknowledging achievements, no matter how small, boosts morale and motivates everyone to continue their path of self-improvement. These celebrations can be simple acknowledgments during meetings or more significant gatherings to commemorate major milestones.

In essence, finding support and accountability is about creating a community that uplifts and motivates, making the journey of growth and transformation a shared and more fulfilling experience. By actively engaging with like-minded individuals, setting up systems of accountability, and utilizing available resources, you can build a strong foundation for sustained growth and lasting change.

Building a Network of Like-Minded People

In the quest for personal growth and transformation, the significance of surrounding oneself with a supportive community cannot be overstated. This network, comprised of individuals who not only share similar goals but also embody the values of mindfulness, resilience, and authenticity, becomes an invaluable resource. The collective energy and wisdom of this group can provide the encouragement needed to overcome obstacles and celebrate successes on the path to self-improvement. Engaging with a community of like-minded individuals offers a unique opportunity to exchange ideas, experiences, and strategies that can enhance one's journey. Through these interactions, members can discover new perspectives and insights, broadening their understanding and approach to personal development.

To effectively build this network, one must be proactive in seeking out groups and forums where these conversations are happening. Whether it's through social media platforms, local community centers, or specialized online forums, the key is to participate actively and genuinely. Sharing one's own experiences and offering support to others not only contributes to the growth of the community but also deepens one's own understanding and commitment to their personal development goals. It's important to approach these interactions with an open heart and mind, ready to both teach and learn, as true growth is a mutual process.

Moreover, the process of building a network of like-minded people should be approached with intentionality. It involves more than just attending meetings or joining online groups; it requires active engagement, regular communication, and the willingness to be vulnerable. Opening up about one's challenges and successes creates a space for authentic connection and mutual support. It's in these spaces that deep, meaningful relationships are forged, relationships that go beyond mere acquaintance and become sources of strength and inspiration.

Collaboration and co-creation with others in your network can also lead to the development of new projects, initiatives, or even accountability groups that further support your growth. These collaborations can take many forms, from joint learning endeavors to co-hosting workshops or webinars that share your collective knowledge and experiences with a wider audience. The act of creating together not only solidifies your network but also amplifies the impact of your shared mission of personal and collective growth.

Remember, the strength of your network lies not just in the number of connections but in the quality of relationships and the shared commitment to support each other's growth. As you continue to engage with and expand your network, remain mindful of the values and goals that brought you together. This mindfulness ensures that your network remains a source of positive energy, inspiration, and mutual support, propelling each member towards their individual and collective goals. Through this network, you not only find companions for your journey but also become a beacon of support and encouragement for others, embodying the very principles of growth, resilience, and transformation you seek to cultivate in your life.

Staying Motivated Through Challenges

Facing challenges is an inevitable part of personal growth and transformation. It's during these times that your inner strength is truly tested, and staying motivated can seem like an uphill battle. However, it's also these moments that offer the greatest opportunities for development and learning. One effective strategy to maintain motivation is to **set small, achievable milestones** within the broader context of your goals. This approach not only makes your journey more manageable but also provides a series of successes that fuel your motivation further. Celebrating these small victories is crucial, as it reinforces the positive progress you're making, no matter how minor it may seem.

Another key aspect of staying motivated through challenges is to **maintain a solution-focused mindset**. When faced with obstacles, instead of dwelling on the problems, shift your focus to finding solutions. This mindset encourages adaptability and creativity, essential qualities for overcoming barriers. It also helps in preventing the feeling of being overwhelmed, as you're actively taking steps to navigate through the difficulties.

Reflecting on past successes can also be incredibly motivating during tough times. Remind yourself of the challenges you've already overcome. This reflection not only boosts your confidence but also serves as a reminder of your resilience and capability to handle adversity. Keeping a journal of your accomplishments and the strategies that helped you achieve them can be a valuable resource to draw upon when faced with new challenges.

Engaging with your support network is another vital strategy. Sharing your struggles and seeking advice or encouragement can provide a fresh perspective and much-needed emotional support. Sometimes, simply knowing that others believe in you can reignite your motivation and drive. Furthermore, your network can offer practical advice and insights that you might not have considered, providing new avenues to overcome your current obstacles.

Lastly, integrating **self-care practices** into your routine is essential for maintaining motivation. Challenges can be draining, both mentally and physically. By ensuring that you're taking care of your well-being, you're better equipped to handle stress and setbacks. Whether it's through exercise, meditation, or pursuing hobbies that bring you joy, self-care is a powerful tool for keeping your spirits high and your motivation intact.

By adopting these strategies, you create a robust framework for staying motivated, regardless of the challenges you may face. Each step forward, no matter how small, is a part of your journey toward growth and transformation. Remember, the essence of building and sustaining motivation through challenges lies in celebrating progress, focusing on solutions, drawing strength from past successes, leaning on your support network, and prioritizing self-care. Through the application of these strategies, you're not only able to navigate through difficult periods but also emerge stronger and more resilient.

Exercise n.25: Accountability Partner Check-In Exercise

Objective: Stay motivated and focused through regular check-ins with an accountability partner.
Type: Accountability Exercise
Duration: Weekly, for at least 20-30 minutes.

Instructions:
Choose an Accountability Partner: Choose a supportive, reliable friend, mentor, or colleague for regular check-ins.

Set a Regular Meeting Time: Schedule a consistent weekly check-in time that suits both of you.

Find a Quiet Space: Choose a calm and comfortable place where you won't be disturbed during your conversation.

Weekly Check-In Agenda: Follow this structure for each check-in:
- Share Goals: Briefly share the goals you set for the week. Discuss whether you achieved them and any obstacles you encountered.
- Celebrate Wins: Take time to celebrate any achievements, no matter how small. Reflect on what went well and why.
- Discuss Challenges: Share challenges and lessons learned. Discuss overcoming similar obstacles in the future.
- Set New Goals: Based on your reflections, set new goals for the upcoming week. Ensure they are realistic and aligned with your long-term objectives.
- Plan Actions: Outline specific actions you will take to achieve your new goals. Identify any resources or support you might need.
- Provide Support: Support your accountability partner by discussing goals, celebrating wins, and navigating challenges.

Document Your Progress: Record weekly check-ins in a notebook, digital document, or journaling app to track progress.

Consistency: Make this accountability check-in exercise a non-negotiable part of your routine to stay motivated and on track.

Conclusion

The essence of personal empowerment and growth lies not just in the acquisition of new knowledge but in the application of this knowledge to everyday life. As you have journeyed through the various chapters and sections of this book, you've encountered a myriad of strategies, exercises, and reflections designed to bolster your inner strength, foster meaningful connections, and cultivate resilience and intentional habits. It's important to remember that the path to lifelong empowerment is not linear. There will be moments of triumph and periods of challenge. The key is to remain committed to your journey, utilizing the tools and insights you've gained to navigate through both the highs and the lows.

Effective personal growth requires a commitment to apply what you've learned consistently. This means integrating mindfulness practices into your daily routine, actively working towards aligning your actions with your core values, and persistently striving to build and maintain authentic relationships. It also involves continuously developing resilient habits, embracing emotional resilience, and cultivating a mindset of gratitude and positivity.

As you move forward, keep in mind the importance of self-reflection. Regularly taking stock of your progress, acknowledging your successes, and identifying areas for improvement will enable you to stay on course and adjust your strategies as needed. Remember, every step you take, no matter how small, is a step towards becoming a more empowered, resilient, and fulfilled individual.

Lastly, never underestimate the power of support and accountability. Surrounding yourself with like-minded individuals who share your commitment to growth can provide an invaluable source of motivation, inspiration, and encouragement. Whether through formal accountability partnerships or informal support networks, these relationships can play a crucial role in helping you sustain your momentum and achieve your goals.

As you continue on your path to lifelong empowerment, remember that the journey itself is as important as the destination. Each experience, whether perceived as positive or negative, offers valuable lessons and opportunities for growth. Stay open, stay committed, and most importantly, stay true to yourself. The journey to forging your inner strength and achieving lasting happiness, intentional habits, and true connections is ongoing, and every day presents a new opportunity to grow, learn, and thrive.

Key Insights and Practices Recap

The foundation of personal empowerment and lifelong growth is built upon **regular self-reflection** and **adjustment**. It's essential to periodically evaluate your progress, celebrate your achievements, and identify areas where you could enhance your approach. This ongoing process of self-assessment ensures that you remain aligned with your core values and purpose, allowing for continued personal development and fulfillment. Furthermore, the significance of **support and accountability** cannot be overstated. Surrounding yourself with a community of like-minded individuals provides not only motivation and inspiration but also a valuable resource for feedback and encouragement. These relationships are instrumental in maintaining momentum towards achieving your goals.

Adapting to change with resilience and a positive mindset is another critical aspect of personal growth. Life is inherently unpredictable, and the ability to navigate through changes with grace and flexibility speaks volumes about your inner strength. Embrace the unknown with an open heart and view each new challenge as an opportunity to learn and expand your horizons. Additionally, **investing in continuous learning** and **skill development** plays a vital role in staying relevant and engaged. Whether through formal education, self-study, or experiential learning, acquiring new knowledge and abilities enriches your life and empowers you to reach new heights.

Practicing self-compassion and **kindness** towards yourself is as important as the effort you put into growing and achieving. Recognize that setbacks and failures are part of the journey and treat yourself with the same empathy and understanding you would offer to a friend in a similar situation. This attitude fosters a healthy relationship with yourself and supports emotional well-being.

Integrating mindfulness into your daily routine is another powerful practice for enhancing self-awareness and emotional intelligence. Mindfulness exercises, such as meditation, deep breathing, or simply being present in the moment, can significantly improve your mental clarity, focus, and stress management. This heightened state of awareness enables you to make more intentional decisions and respond to life's challenges with calmness and clarity.

Cultivating gratitude and focusing on the positive aspects of your life can dramatically shift your perspective and overall happiness. Taking time each day to reflect on what you're thankful for encourages a positive mindset and helps to counteract the negativity bias that is so common in our thought processes.

Building and maintaining healthy habits— ranging from regular physical activity and balanced nutrition to adequate sleep and relaxation—lays the foundation for physical and mental well-being. These habits support your body's needs, boost your energy levels, and enhance your ability to focus and perform at your best.

Setting clear, achievable goals that are aligned with your values and purpose not only provides direction but also a sense of accomplishment as you progress towards them. Break larger goals into smaller, manageable tasks to maintain motivation and momentum. Celebrating small wins along the way reinforces your commitment and enthusiasm for the journey ahead.

Remember, the essence of personal empowerment lies in the consistent application of these practices and insights. By committing to this path of self-improvement and drawing upon the support and resources available to you, you are well-equipped to navigate the complexities of life with resilience, purpose, and joy. Engage with each day as an opportunity to learn, grow, and contribute, keeping in mind that every experience, interaction, and challenge offers valuable lessons and opportunities for personal development.

The Journey Forward

Engaging with each day as an opportunity to learn, grow, and contribute, keeping in mind that every experience, interaction, and challenge offers valuable lessons and opportunities for personal development is a cornerstone of embracing your empowered self. This mindset not only propels you forward in your personal journey but also enriches your life with depth, meaning, and fulfillment. It's crucial to approach each day with curiosity and an eagerness to uncover what lies ahead, ready to embrace both the successes and the obstacles that come your way. This proactive stance towards life encourages a dynamic and responsive approach to personal growth, where you are continually adapting, learning, and evolving.

Cultivating a proactive approach to challenges involves recognizing that obstacles are not setbacks but rather opportunities for growth and learning. This shift in perspective requires a conscious effort to reframe challenges as stepping stones rather than roadblocks. By adopting this mindset, you empower yourself to navigate life's ups and downs with resilience and grace, always looking for the lesson or the silver lining in difficult situations.

Embracing vulnerability as a strength is another vital aspect of your journey forward. Allowing yourself to be vulnerable, to share your struggles, and to ask for help when needed is a sign of strength and self-awareness. It opens the door to deeper connections with others and fosters a supportive environment where growth can flourish. Vulnerability is the foundation upon which trust and authenticity are built, both with yourself and with others.

Practicing gratitude on a daily basis is a powerful tool for maintaining a positive outlook and fostering happiness. By taking time each day to reflect on the things you are thankful for, you shift your focus from what you lack to what you have, cultivating an abundance mindset. This practice not only enhances your emotional well-being but also attracts more positivity into your life, creating a virtuous cycle of gratitude and contentment.

Investing in relationships that uplift and support you is essential for sustaining your journey of growth and transformation. Surrounding yourself with people who inspire, challenge, and encourage you is invaluable. These relationships provide a source of strength, motivation, and comfort as you navigate the complexities of life. They also offer a mirror through which you can see yourself more clearly, helping you to grow into your best self.

Committing to lifelong learning ensures that you remain open, adaptable, and curious. The world is constantly changing, and there is always something new to discover. By embracing a mindset of continuous learning, you equip yourself with the tools necessary to navigate the future, whatever it may hold. This commitment to growth and development is a testament to your resilience and your determination to live a life of purpose and fulfillment.

Taking care of your physical well-being through regular exercise, proper nutrition, and sufficient rest is foundational to maintaining the energy and vitality needed for personal growth. Your physical health is deeply intertwined with your mental and emotional well-being, and by prioritizing self-care, you ensure that you are at your best, ready to face whatever challenges come your way.

Fostering a sense of curiosity and wonder about the world around you keeps the journey exciting and engaging. There is beauty and intrigue in the everyday, and by cultivating an attitude of wonder, you open yourself up to the joy and awe that life has to offer. This sense of curiosity fuels your creativity, sparks your imagination, and keeps you motivated to explore, learn, and grow.

Celebrating your achievements, no matter how small, reinforces your sense of accomplishment and boosts your confidence. Acknowledging your progress and taking pride in your successes is crucial for maintaining motivation and momentum on your journey. These celebrations are reminders of how far you've come and serve as encouragement to continue pushing forward, setting new goals, and reaching new heights.

By integrating these practices into your daily life, you actively participate in shaping a future that reflects your deepest values, aspirations, and potentials. The journey forward is an ongoing process of becoming, a dynamic and ever-evolving path that leads to a more empowered, resilient, and fulfilled self. Through commitment, resilience, and an open heart, you are well-equipped to embrace the challenges and opportunities that lie ahead, forging a life of purpose, meaning, and joy.

Resources for Learning and Growth

To further your journey of self-improvement and inner strength, a variety of resources are available that cater to the diverse needs and preferences of readers. These include:

- **Books and Audiobooks**: For those who seek depth and comprehensive understanding, books such as "The Power of Now" by Eckhart Tolle and "Mindset: The New Psychology of Success" by Carol S. Dweck provide profound insights into mindfulness and the growth mindset. Audiobooks offer the convenience of learning on the go, making them a great option for busy individuals.

- **Podcasts**: Podcasts like "The Tim Ferriss Show" and "On Being with Krista Tippett" feature conversations with thought leaders and experts in various fields. These discussions can offer new perspectives and practical advice on personal development, resilience, and living a fulfilled life.

- **Online Courses**: Websites like Coursera and Udemy offer courses on a wide range of topics, including personal development, mindfulness, and emotional intelligence. These platforms provide the flexibility to learn at your own pace and often include interactive exercises and community forums for discussion.

- **Meditation Apps**: Apps such as Headspace and Calm offer guided meditations, mindfulness exercises, and sleep stories to help reduce stress and improve overall well-being. These tools can be particularly useful for incorporating daily mindfulness practices into your routine.

- **Support Groups and Workshops**: Local and online support groups and workshops can provide a sense of community and shared learning. Participating in these groups offers the opportunity to connect with others on similar paths, share experiences, and learn from each other.

- **Professional Coaching**: For personalized guidance, professional life coaches can work with you to set goals, develop strategies, and overcome obstacles. Coaching can be a valuable resource for those looking for tailored support and accountability.

Each of these resources can complement the practices and insights shared in this book, offering additional avenues for growth and learning. By exploring these options, you can continue to build on the foundation of inner strength and empowerment cultivated through your reading and reflections.

The Phases of Personal Growth

Now we reached the end of this book, and it's important to remember that personal growth unfolds in stages, much like learning to drive a car.

These phases guide us through the journey of self-improvement, each building on the last.

Phase 1: "Unaware of Areas for Improvement"
At first, we may not see what we need to improve, just as a beginner doesn't yet grasp the full skill set required for driving.

Phase 2: "Recognizing the Need to Learn"
Next, we realize there's a gap between where we are and where we want to be, motivating us to seek growth.

Phase 3: "Identifying Specific Areas to Improve"
As we delve deeper, we pinpoint the exact skills or habits to work on, similar to a learner driver mastering the basics.

Phase 4: "Building Confidence Through Practice"
With ongoing practice, our new skills start to show. We begin to see real progress and feel a growing sense of confidence.

Phase 5: "Operating with Ease and Mastery"
Finally, growth becomes natural and effortless, just as driving does over time. Our new habits are fully integrated into who we are.

As you continue to *forge your inner strength*, remember that growth is a cycle.

Each phase, even the challenging ones, brings you closer to the person you're becoming.

Personal growth isn't a one-time achievement; it's a process that adds depth and meaning to every stage of life.

Final Reflection Exercise

Objective: Think back on what you've accomplished thus far and make plans for future development.
Type: Closing Reflection Exercise
Duration: One-time session, for at least 30-45 minutes.

Instructions:
Set Aside Time: Dedicate 30-45 minutes for this exercise. Choose a time when you can reflect deeply without interruptions.

Find a Quiet Space: Choose a calm and comfortable place where you won't be disturbed.

Final Reflection Prompts: Answer the following prompts to reflect on your journey and set future intentions:
* Reflect on Your Path: Look back on the period of personal growth and development you've undergone. Write down key moments, achievements, and challenges you faced.
* Celebrate Achievements: Identify and celebrate significant achievements. Reflect on what went well and why these accomplishments are meaningful to you.
* Assess Challenges: Reflect on any challenges or setbacks you encountered. Consider what you learned from these experiences and how they contributed to your growth.
* Identify Personal Growth: Reflect on areas where you have experienced personal growth. Write down specific skills, habits, or behaviors that have improved.
* Set Future Intentions: Based on your reflections, set intentions for future growth. Identify areas you want to continue developing and write down specific goals or actions you will take.
* Express Gratitude: Write down three things you are grateful for in your journey. This helps reinforce a positive mindset and appreciation for your progress.

Document Your Reflections: Use a notebook, a digital document, or a journaling app to record your final reflections. This will help you track your journey and set a foundation for future growth.

My Preferred Books

The following books must be in your library. Each of these authors is an institution and has contributed greatly to personal growth. Each author's strengths will be discussed in the next chapter. I'll just give you this table for now to have the full list. This list is "my" list—other authors could have been included—but these have shaped my life. If you can find out what they're about after reading the next chapter, read them in any order.

Author	Famous Books / Contributions
Earl Nightingale	*The Strangest Secret* *Lead the Field*
Napoleon Hill	*Think and Grow Rich* *The Law of Success* *Outwitting the Devil*
Norman Vincent Peale	*The Power of Positive Thinking* *The Positive Principle Today*
Jim Rohn	*The Art of Exceptional Living* *Seven Strategies for Wealth and Happiness*
Zig Ziglar	*See You at the Top* *Born to Win* *Better Than Good*
Brian Tracy	*Goals!* *Eat That Frog!* *The Psychology of Achievement*
Bob Proctor	*You Were Born Rich* Contributions to *The Secret*

Pioneers in Personal Growth

T here was a time in my life when I felt stuck—
caught in a cycle of self-doubt and hesitation. I
knew I had potential, but I didn't have a clear idea of
how to tap into it. I wanted to be stronger, more
resilient, and fully in control of my decisions, but I
didn't always know where to start.

During those times, turning to the wisdom of certain
remarkable people became a lifeline for me. These were
thinkers who had not only studied personal growth but
had lived it. They had faced their own setbacks, asked
hard questions, and found powerful ways to move
forward.

In this chapter, I'd like to introduce you to some of
these people who helped me find my way when I
needed it most. Each of them has left behind a legacy of
insights that are practical, real, and surprisingly easy to
apply.

What struck me most about their work was how deeply
it resonated with my own experiences and struggles.
Their words felt like personal advice, almost as if they

understood exactly what I was going through. From the power of positive thinking to setting meaningful goals, these pioneers helped me realize that change wasn't as complicated as I had imagined.

As you read about their ideas, I hope you'll find the same encouragement and clarity I did. These teachings aren't abstract theories—they're tools you can start using today to build a life that feels strong, purposeful, and fully yours.

Earl Nightingale: The Power of Thought and Purpose

When I first encountered Earl Nightingale's work, it was like a light bulb went off. Here was someone who spoke about the power of our thoughts with such conviction and clarity that I couldn't ignore it. Nightingale is often called the "Dean of Personal Development," and it's easy to see why. His central message—that *"we become what we think about"*—sounds simple, but once I truly understood it, I realized it had the potential to change everything. At that time, I was going through a period of doubt. I knew I wanted to achieve more, but my mind seemed full of reasons why I couldn't. Nightingale's words made me stop and reflect: what if I was unintentionally holding myself back by focusing on these limitations?

In his landmark recording, *The Strangest Secret*, Nightingale explains that our minds are incredibly powerful, and that by focusing our thoughts, we have the ability to shape our own reality. This idea of "thinking with purpose" was completely new to me. Before, I had let my mind wander wherever it wanted, often toward worries, fears, and doubts. But Nightingale's message encouraged me to take control. I decided to test his approach by setting a clear goal and focusing my thoughts on it daily.

Each morning, I would spend just a few minutes visualizing myself as the person I wanted to become—stronger, more resilient, and in control of my life. I imagined specific situations where I would act with confidence, where I would overcome challenges calmly, and I'd picture myself succeeding in ways that felt meaningful to me. At first, it felt a bit strange, almost too simple. But over time, I noticed that these brief moments of focused thought were making a real difference. I was more energized and started taking actions that aligned with my vision, rather than getting caught up in hesitation or doubt.

Nightingale also emphasized the importance of setting clear goals, something I hadn't given much thought to before. He believed that having a defined purpose keeps our minds focused and grounded. Inspired by this, I took time to write down a few specific goals, things I wanted to achieve within a year. By keeping these goals in the forefront of my mind, I found myself making decisions that supported them, even subconsciously. Instead of drifting through my days, I had a clearer sense of direction, and my daily actions started to reflect that purpose.

What I find truly unique about Nightingale's work is its practicality. He doesn't just tell you to "think positively" in an abstract way. He gives you a process: visualize your goals, focus on them consistently, and watch as your thoughts begin to shape your actions. This isn't about ignoring reality or pretending problems don't exist; it's about choosing to put energy into thoughts that move you forward. The more I practiced this, the more I noticed small but significant changes in my life. I began handling challenges with a bit more confidence and approaching setbacks as temporary, rather than insurmountable.

For anyone who feels stuck or overwhelmed, Nightingale's work offers a refreshing approach. It teaches that the real power lies in controlling our minds, not our circumstances. By choosing thoughts that align with the reality we want to create, we start building a life that feels intentional and fulfilling. Nightingale taught me that I'm not just a passive participant in my life—I'm actively creating it, one thought at a time. His insights were the first steps in helping me take control of my mindset and understand that, truly, our thoughts are the foundation of everything we achieve.

Napoleon Hill: The Power of Desire and Faith

If Earl Nightingale helped me understand the power of thought, then Napoleon Hill took it a step further by teaching me the value of *desire* and *faith* as driving forces for achievement. Hill's work, particularly in his book *Think and Grow Rich*, explores the idea that success begins with a deeply felt desire—a goal so strong it becomes almost a burning obsession. I remember reading his words during a time when I felt disconnected from my goals, almost as if they were just ideas floating around without any real urgency. Hill's concept of desire, however, gave me a new sense of purpose.

Hill spent years studying successful people and identified "definiteness of purpose" as the foundation of achievement. He encouraged readers to focus on a single, well-defined goal with unwavering faith. Inspired by this, I decided to get specific about my own goals, breaking them down from vague wishes into concrete plans. I would write down my main goal every day, just as Hill recommended, as a way to keep it in my mind and make it feel real. This daily ritual felt strange at first, but over time, I noticed that my goal started to feel less like a dream and more like something tangible that I could achieve.

Hill also introduced me to the concept of the "mastermind," which he described as a group of like-minded individuals who support each other's growth and success. This idea resonated with me because I had often tried to tackle my goals alone. I decided to reach out to a few friends who were also pursuing personal growth, and we began meeting regularly to discuss our progress, share advice, and hold each other accountable. I quickly discovered that surrounding myself with supportive people amplified my motivation and kept me on track, just as Hill had promised.

One of Hill's greatest insights is the importance of *faith* in our ability to succeed. He wasn't talking about faith in a religious sense, but rather a firm belief in our own potential to achieve our desires. Hill taught that by visualizing our success and affirming our confidence, we strengthen our belief that we can make it happen. For me, this meant shifting from thoughts like "I hope I can do this" to "I know I can do this." That small but powerful shift in language began to change the way I viewed my own abilities.

Hill's work is unique in that it doesn't just focus on the practical steps to success, but also on the emotional and mental commitment required to achieve it. He believed that success starts within—a combination of desire, faith, and persistence. By instilling these qualities in myself, I found I could overcome setbacks with a sense of determination I hadn't felt before. *Think and Grow Rich* became more than just a book for me; it was a guide for building an unshakable belief in my own potential. Hill taught me that when desire and faith are aligned, they form a powerful force that drives us toward our goals, no matter the obstacles in our path.

Norman Vincent Peale: Positive Thinking for Fulfillment

As I continued exploring the mindset behind success, Norman Vincent Peale's work taught me something equally valuable: the power of positivity in shaping not just our achievements, but our overall sense of well-being. Peale is best known for his book *The Power of Positive Thinking*, which became a classic because it showed readers that optimism isn't just a feel-good idea; it's a tool for transforming our lives. When I first read Peale's words, I realized how often my own thoughts had been colored by doubt and negativity. He made me see that to create a life of fulfillment, I had to start by cultivating a positive outlook.

Peale believed that our thoughts directly affect our reality, and that by choosing positive beliefs, we could overcome almost any challenge. I remember a time when I felt overwhelmed by a series of setbacks and disappointments. Peale's teachings encouraged me to shift my focus from what was going wrong to what could go right. I began using affirmations, as he suggested, repeating phrases like "I am capable and resilient" and "I can handle anything that comes my way." At first, these affirmations felt almost too simple to be effective. But as I practiced them daily, I noticed that my inner dialogue started to change. Instead of immediately expecting the worst, I found myself looking for solutions, feeling more hopeful and energized.

One of the most powerful ideas I took from Peale is that positive thinking isn't about ignoring problems; it's about facing them with a mindset that empowers you rather than one that defeats you. Peale encouraged readers to practice gratitude and to focus on what's going well, even when life feels difficult. I tried this by writing down three things I was grateful for every morning. Some days, these were small things—a warm cup of coffee, a kind word from a friend. Other days, they were moments of clarity or small victories. This practice of gratitude helped me build resilience, giving me the strength to see beyond immediate challenges.

Peale's work blends psychology with spirituality, creating a holistic approach that makes his teachings feel grounded and accessible. He believed that faith and positive thinking go hand-in-hand, and that by trusting in ourselves and a higher purpose, we find the courage to persevere. I found that his ideas about faith resonated with me deeply. Whenever I doubted myself, I would remind myself of his words about self-belief and trust. Peale's work gave me a framework to lean on when I felt uncertain, a reminder that optimism is a choice we can make, even in hard times.

In many ways, Peale's teachings brought me back to a place of hope and strength. They reminded me that no matter the situation, I have the power to choose a mindset that lifts me up. His work taught me that positive thinking isn't just a tool for success; it's a foundation for a fulfilling, resilient life. Through his guidance, I came to understand that by changing our thoughts, we truly can change our world.

Jim Rohn: Personal Responsibility and Character-Building

While exploring the principles of success, I encountered Jim Rohn's teachings, and they struck a chord with me in a way I hadn't expected. Rohn's philosophy centers around personal responsibility and character-building, reminding us that lasting success isn't just about external achievements—it's about who we become in the process. One of Rohn's most memorable teachings is, *"Success is something you attract by the person you become."* At a time when I was frustrated by the slow pace of my progress, Rohn's words helped me see that true growth happens within and that developing my character was just as important as reaching any goal.

Rohn believed that success is built on the foundation of discipline, consistency, and self-reflection. Inspired by this, I began focusing on small, daily habits that aligned with my values. I realized that I had often overlooked the power of seemingly simple actions—waking up a bit earlier, planning my day, and making time for self-reflection. Following Rohn's advice, I made these habits a priority, recognizing that they were shaping not only my days but also my character. Slowly, I started noticing that these small disciplines were creating a ripple effect, impacting my confidence and my sense of purpose.

One of the most transformative concepts Rohn introduced to me was the idea of *taking complete responsibility* for my life. He taught that blaming circumstances or other people is a way of giving up our power. Instead, Rohn encouraged a mindset of accountability, urging us to focus on what we can control. This message came to me at a time when I was feeling discouraged and was quick to point fingers at outside factors for my setbacks. Rohn's perspective challenged me to look inward and ask myself what I could do differently. Taking ownership of my choices and actions was empowering. It taught me that, while I couldn't control everything around me, I could always choose how I responded.

Rohn also emphasized the importance of surrounding ourselves with people who inspire us. He famously said, *"You are the average of the five people you spend the most time with."* Reflecting on this, I took a hard look at my circle and realized that I wasn't always around those who lifted me up. Motivated by Rohn's advice, I made a conscious effort to seek out positive influences—people who were driven, optimistic, and aligned with the values I wanted to embody. This change in my environment reinforced my goals and provided the encouragement I needed during challenging times.

What sets Rohn apart is his down-to-earth wisdom. He doesn't offer shortcuts; instead, he shows us that the path to success lies in developing character and taking responsibility for our lives. His teachings helped me understand that success is not a destination but a reflection of the habits and values we cultivate. Through Rohn's guidance, I learned that real achievement is measured not only by what we accomplish but by who we become along the way. His words are a reminder that personal growth is an ongoing process, one that requires patience, dedication, and a commitment to becoming our best selves.

Zig Ziglar: Motivation and Faith-Based Success

Zig Ziglar's work brought something into my life that I hadn't fully appreciated until then—motivation fueled by faith and positivity. Known for his uplifting speeches and engaging storytelling, Ziglar was a master at inspiring others to reach for their best, not just in what they do but in who they are. Reading his words and listening to his talks gave me a renewed sense of hope and energy during a period when I was feeling stagnant and unmotivated. Ziglar had a way of reminding me that every day is a new opportunity to improve, to grow, and to create a life filled with purpose.

Ziglar taught that a successful mindset is grounded in positivity and integrity. He famously said, *"You don't have to be great to start, but you have to start to be great."* Those words came to me just when I was hesitating to take on new challenges, weighed down by fears of not being "good enough." His message encouraged me to focus less on perfection and more on just taking that first step. I realized that, like so many people, I had been waiting for the "right moment" to pursue my goals. Ziglar's teachings showed me that the right moment is simply the one we choose, and that every small step taken with faith leads us closer to our potential.

One thing that set Ziglar apart was his faith-based approach to success. For him, success wasn't just about personal gain; it was about living with integrity, treating others with respect, and staying true to one's values. This idea resonated deeply with me. Ziglar believed that true success must be built on a foundation of strong morals and a positive attitude, not just ambition. This focus on values helped me see that success isn't just measured by accomplishments—it's about how we reach them and the kind of person we become along the way. Ziglar encouraged me to look at my goals from a broader perspective, one that includes the quality of my character and the relationships I build.

Ziglar also emphasized the importance of self-belief, often reminding his audience that, *"If you can dream it, you can achieve it."* Inspired by this, I began to take my dreams more seriously, treating them as goals rather than distant ideas. Ziglar's confidence in human potential felt contagious; he had a way of making you believe that your dreams were within reach, as long as you were willing to work for them. He helped me understand that self-belief isn't just about feeling capable; it's about having the faith to pursue your dreams with all your heart.

What I love most about Ziglar's work is its warmth and optimism. His storytelling made his advice feel relatable and actionable, not some distant ideal. He taught me that motivation isn't just a one-time boost— it's a daily commitment to living with purpose, positivity, and perseverance. Through Ziglar's teachings, I found that the combination of faith, integrity, and a positive mindset isn't just a pathway to success; it's a way of life that brings meaning and fulfillment. His words remind me that we all have the power to shape our lives, and that with the right attitude, there's no limit to what we can achieve.

Brian Tracy: Goal-Setting and Time Management

Brian Tracy's work taught me the power of goal-setting and time management, and it's hard to overstate just how much this has transformed my life. Tracy has a talent for breaking down success into clear, actionable steps, which was exactly what I needed when I first encountered his teachings. At that time, I had a lot of dreams but little structure in place to turn them into reality. Tracy's approach was refreshingly practical, giving me a roadmap that I could follow to make meaningful progress each day.

One of Tracy's core teachings is the importance of setting specific, written goals. He encouraged readers to take the time to define exactly what they want and to write it down—a simple act that has profound effects. Following his advice, I began writing out my goals each morning, clearly articulating what I wanted to achieve in my career, relationships, and personal growth. This practice gave me a sense of direction that I hadn't felt before, and it kept me focused on what really mattered. Tracy's method helped me turn vague aspirations into concrete targets, making each goal feel not only achievable but inevitable, as long as I stayed committed.

Tracy is also known for his focus on time management, especially his famous advice to *"Eat That Frog!"*—a metaphor for tackling the most important or challenging task first. This was a game-changer for me. Like many people, I used to spend my days busy but not necessarily productive, often procrastinating on tasks that felt overwhelming. Tracy's advice to tackle the toughest job first helped me overcome that tendency. By taking on my hardest tasks early in the day, I found that my productivity skyrocketed, and the rest of my day felt easier and more rewarding. This shift in my routine made me realize just how powerful it is to start each day with purpose and intention.

Another lesson I took from Tracy was the value of continuous learning. He taught that to be successful, we should treat our minds like a "never-ending project," always seeking to expand our skills and knowledge. Inspired by this, I committed to reading more, attending seminars, and seeking out opportunities for growth. Tracy's emphasis on lifelong learning reminded me that progress doesn't stop once we reach our goals— there's always more to learn, more to achieve, and more ways to improve ourselves.

Tracy's approach is practical, straightforward, and results-driven, and that's what makes his teachings so accessible. He doesn't rely on abstract ideas; instead, he gives clear steps to help you take control of your time, define your goals, and move steadily toward success. His strategies are designed to empower you to make the most of every day, encouraging a disciplined approach that brings clarity and efficiency to everything you do.

Tracy's influence on my life is evident not only in the goals I've achieved but in the way I approach each day, making each moment count.

Through Tracy's teachings, I learned that success isn't about talent or luck—it's about having a plan and following through with consistency. His methods helped me develop the habits and mindset necessary to achieve lasting success. Tracy's work serves as a reminder that when we take control of our time and define our goals with purpose, we gain the ability to create a life that truly reflects our aspirations.

Bob Proctor: The Law of Attraction and Self-Belief

Bob Proctor's teachings introduced me to the power of the subconscious mind and the concept of the law of attraction. Known for his work in *The Secret* and his own book, *You Were Born Rich*, Proctor's approach goes beyond traditional goal-setting and delves into the power of self-belief and visualization in creating a life we desire. When I first came across Proctor's ideas, I was intrigued by the emphasis he placed on the connection between our beliefs and the reality we experience. He taught that if we want to achieve something extraordinary, we have to start by transforming the way we see ourselves.

One of Proctor's most impactful teachings for me was the idea that we are only limited by our self-image. He explained that our subconscious mind holds deep-seated beliefs that influence our behaviors and ultimately shape our outcomes. This realization hit me hard. I began to reflect on my own self-image and realized that, like so many others, I had been carrying around limiting beliefs—ideas that told me I wasn't capable enough or that my goals were out of reach. Proctor's approach gave me the tools to challenge these beliefs and replace them with empowering ones.

Proctor introduced me to the practice of visualization, encouraging people to vividly imagine their goals as if they had already been achieved. Inspired by this, I began to set aside time each day to visualize my desired future, seeing myself as successful, confident, and fulfilled. At first, it felt strange, but I soon discovered that visualization was a powerful way to reinforce positive beliefs. By picturing myself achieving my goals, I was training my mind to recognize opportunities and take actions that aligned with my aspirations. Proctor often said, *"See yourself already in possession of your goal,"* and that simple practice shifted how I approached each day.

Affirmations were another key tool I took from Proctor's teachings. He believed that by repeating positive, present-tense statements, we could reprogram our minds to believe in our potential. I started creating my own affirmations, like "I am worthy of success" and "I have the power to create the life I want." Repeating these affirmations daily helped to strengthen my self-belief, especially during challenging times. Proctor taught me that self-belief isn't just about feeling confident; it's about reshaping our internal narrative so that it aligns with the life we want to create.

What sets Proctor apart is his profound belief in human potential and his conviction that we can change our lives by changing our mindset. His focus on the subconscious mind and the law of attraction offers a unique approach that encourages us to think beyond what we see and to trust in our ability to manifest what we desire. Proctor's teachings reminded me that our thoughts are like seeds planted in the subconscious; with consistent nurturing through belief, visualization, and action, they grow into tangible results.

Through Proctor's guidance, I learned that success isn't solely about effort—it's about believing in yourself, challenging your limitations, and aligning your inner world with the life you want. His work is a testament to the power of the mind, showing that when we believe deeply in our potential, we can create a reality that reflects our highest aspirations.

Conclusion: A Legacy of Inner Strength and Success

As I reflect on the insights and lessons from these incredible thinkers, I realize that each one has contributed something unique to my own path of personal growth. **Earl Nightingale** taught me the immense power of thought and how aligning our minds with our goals can reshape our reality. **Napoleon Hill** helped me understand the importance of desire and faith, showing me that success is born from a deep-seated determination and a clear purpose. **Norman Vincent Peale** gave me the gift of positive thinking, teaching me that optimism and gratitude are powerful tools for overcoming challenges and finding fulfillment. **Jim Rohn's** emphasis on personal responsibility and character-building reminded me that true success is measured not only by what we achieve but by who we become. **Zig Ziglar** inspired me with his message of motivation and integrity, encouraging me to pursue my goals with faith and kindness. **Brian Tracy** showed me the power of structure and discipline, helping me understand that setting goals and managing time are essential steps on the path to achievement. And finally, **Bob Proctor** introduced me to the transformative potential of self-belief and visualization, teaching me that our minds are limitless, capable of manifesting the life we truly desire.

Each of these pioneers offers a different perspective, yet together they form a comprehensive guide for anyone looking to build inner strength and live with purpose. They taught me that personal growth isn't about shortcuts or overnight success; it's about daily commitment, resilience, and a willingness to look within. Their teachings remind us that real change starts from the inside, from the thoughts we choose, the beliefs we hold, and the actions we take every day.

As you take these insights and make them your own, I hope you'll feel the same sense of possibility and empowerment that they brought to me. These lessons are more than just theories—they're tools you can use to shape a life that feels authentic and fulfilling. Remember, this journey of growth and self-discovery is ongoing, filled with challenges but also incredible rewards. The wisdom of these pioneers is here to guide you, helping you become the person you've always envisioned. Take these teachings to heart, apply them to your life, and watch as you unlock your true potential, step by step.

Made in United States
Orlando, FL
12 December 2024